Editor-in-Chief and Founder:
  Lyndon H. LaRouche, Jr.
Editorial Board: *Lyndon H. LaRouche, Jr. , Helga Zepp-LaRouche, Robert Ingraham, Tony Papert, Gerald Rose, Dennis Small, Jeffrey Steinberg, William Wertz*
Co-Editors: *Robert Ingraham, Tony Papert*
Managing Editor: *Nancy Spannaus*
Technology: *Marsha Freeman*
Books: *Katherine Notley*
Ebooks: *Richard Burden*
Graphics: *Alan Yue*
Photos: *Stuart Lewis*
Circulation Manager: *Stanley Ezrol*

INTELLIGENCE DIRECTORS
Counterintelligence: *Jeffrey Steinberg, Michele Steinberg*
Economics: *John Hoefle, Marcia Merry Baker, Paul Gallagher*
History: *Anton Chaitkin*
Ibero-America: *Dennis Small*
Russia and Eastern Europe: *Rachel Douglas*
United States: *Debra Freeman*

INTERNATIONAL BUREAUS
Bogotá: *Miriam Redondo*
Berlin: *Rainer Apel*
Copenhagen: *Tom Gillesberg*
Houston: *Harley Schlanger*
Lima: *Sara Madueño*
Melbourne: *Robert Barwick*
Mexico City: *Gerardo Castilleja Chávez*
New Delhi: *Ramtanu Maitra*
Paris: *Christine Bierre*
Stockholm: *Ulf Sandmark*
United Nations, N.Y.C.: *Leni Rubinstein*
Washington, D.C.: *William Jones*
Wiesbaden: *Göran Haglund*

ON THE WEB
e-mail: eirns@larouchepub.com
www.larouchepub.com
www.executiveintelligencereview.com
www.larouchepub.com/eiw
Webmaster: *John Sigerson*
Assistant Webmaster: *George Hollis*
Editor, Arabic-language edition: *Hussein Askary*

EIR (ISSN 0273-6314) *is published weekly (50 issues), by EIR News Service, Inc., P.O. Box 17390, Washington, D.C. 20041-0390. (703) 297-8434*

European Headquarters: E.I.R. GmbH, Postfach Bahnstrasse 9a, D-65205, Wiesbaden, Germany
Tel: 49-611-73650
Homepage: http://www.eir.de
e-mail: info@eir.de
Director: Georg Neudecker

Montreal, Canada: 514-461-1557
eir@eircanada.ca

Denmark: EIR - Danmark, Sankt Knuds Vej 11, basement left, DK-1903 Frederiksberg, Denmark. Tel.: +45 35 43 60 40, Fax: +45 35 43 87 57. e-mail: eirdk@hotmail.com.

Mexico City: EIR, Sor Juana Inés de la Cruz 242-2 Col. Agricultura C.P. 11360 Delegación M. Hidalgo, México D.F. Tel. (5525) 5318-2301
eirmexico@gmail.com

One Unified National Mission

HARVEY DISASTER MADE BY WALL STREET

LaRouche Issues Emergency Plan of Action

Aug. 31—The catastrophe in Texas is a man-made disaster accomplished by the criminal negligence of this nation's elected officials who have continued to support Wall Street's speculative economy and imperial ambitions, while arguing that the nation cannot afford to rebuild and replace its ancient and broken-down economic infrastructure. For the third time since 2005, major American cities have been flooded and their people devastated, because the plans for new infrastructure to protect the people, requiring tens of billions in investments, have been ignored and turned down. Hurricane Harvey now looms as the worst national disaster in our nation's history, and it is a disaster which did not have to happen.

In 2005, Hurricane Katrina killed nearly 2,000 people and wreaked $130 billion in economic losses. Only then, slowly, new flood-control and seagate infrastructure was built—at last—for New Orleans, at a fraction of the human and monetary costs of the damage inflicted by the storm. How many unnecessary deaths and how much suffering could this project have averted?

Four years later, the American Society of Civil Engineers met in Manhattan to discuss several storm surge barrier options for the New York City region. The estimate for the largest of these was $9 billion. The government decided to do nothing. Then, in 2012 Superstorm Sandy killed more than 100 people and caused $65 billion in economic losses. New York area residents are now going through a "Summer of Hell," as the 100-year-old regional transportation system, flooded and damaged five years ago, also was not repaired or replaced at the necessary pace.

The staggering economic and human suffering caused by Hurricane Harvey in the Texas and Louisiana Gulf region are not yet known, and will grow in magnitude as the water recedes; but, what has been known for many years, is that Texas Gulf cities are flood-prone, and have been repeatedly flooded. Yet, no flood control or storm protection infrastructure has been built since the end of World War II. Plans for a new system for the Houston area had been drafted, but their $25 billion cost was deemed "too high" a price tag for our Wall Street–dominated agencies and elected officials. Now, hundreds of billions of dollars, and priceless human lives, are lost.

All of these disasters, and others in the recent period, could have been averted for a fraction of their eventual cost in lost wealth, let alone in lost lives. The media insist to Americans that each city's disaster is caused by its particular economic habits, its choice of location, its squabbling jurisdictions, its ignoring of climate change, or its being close to water! This is nonsense. Wall Street, which has been bailed out repeatedly to the tune of trillions of dollars, with nothing but increased impoverishment of the American people to show for it, must no longer be allowed to dictate the economic policy of the United States of America.

"The nation calls for action, and action now!" in President Franklin Roosevelt's words. During his presidency, and through the 1940s, the new infrastructure to prevent such "natural disasters" —such as the Tennessee Valley Authority—was funded by national credit, as through the Reconstruction Finance Corporation and the Works Progress Administration.

Hurricane Harvey's drowning of cities in East Texas should be the national alarm which ends 70 years in which the country has been without any such national credit institutions.

A Sea-Change Is Required

On August 30, Lyndon LaRouche called for a "sea change" in policy "right now." He called for the immediate creation of a national credit institution for new, high-technology infrastructure, like that employed by Roosevelt when the vast majority of our current infrastructure was built. There is no alternative to creating a national credit institution, like that employed by Alexander Hamilton in accord with our Constitution, to fund the necessary trillions in new infrastructure investment.

There must also be action to reinstate Glass-Steagall banking separation right now, as a new financial crisis looms and Wall Street speculation continues to prevent actual productive investment. Allowing Wall Street to eliminate the Glass-Steagall Act in the 1990s, led to a crash that caused $10 trillion in lost wealth, mass unemployment, and untold loss and shortening of human lives.

LaRouche insists that his "Four Economic Laws to Save the Nation" must be implemented right now if this country is to recover from Hurricane Harvey and prevent similar disasters stemming from our rotting physical economy now ticking like a time bomb:

• Re-institute Glass-Steagall: break up Wall Street and its power;

• Create national credit institutions based on FDR's Reconstruction Finance Corporation and Alexander Hamilton's national banks;

• Invest the credit in new infrastructure using frontier technologies, including high-speed rail, fourth-generation fission and fusion power technologies, and modern storm protection and water management systems;

• Adopt a fusion-driver "crash program": let a great expansion of NASA space exploration provide a driver for productivity and productive employment.

A New Paradigm Takes Hold

China's Belt and Road Initiative, an international program of new rail "land-bridges" and great projects of infrastructural development, offers immediate cooperation for the credit and the building of a new infrastructure in the United States. This initiative is now moving on great projects long identified as absolutely essential, such as the Kra Canal in Southeast Asia and the revival of Lake Chad in sub-Saharan Africa, projects long championed by Lyndon LaRouche and his wife, Helga Zepp-LaRouche.

Helga and Lyndon LaRouche are leading a national mobilization focused on moving President Trump to immediately bring America into the China-initiated Belt and Road Initiative of worldwide building of new infrastructure. That "win-win" initiative, and the United States joining in its worldwide projects and also building its own new infrastructure, means the revival of the United States as an industrial power.

On August 26, Helga Zepp-LaRouche addressed a Manhattan conference on the infrastructure emergency in the United States, making the following proposal: *"Just think what enormous potential will open up if the United States would cooperate with the Belt and Road Initiative,"* Zepp-LaRouche told the conference. *"I think it is really important to imagine a completely different system. If the United States would now do what Franklin D. Roosevelt did—a New Deal, Glass-Steagall, cooperate with China—the United States could experience an industrial revolution bigger than any time in its own history. People just have to grasp that we are right now at the end of a system, a system which cannot be saved. We need to replace it with a completely new system, and most people have just a hard time to imagine that, but there are examples of such changes. The Marshall Plan in Europe was such an example, and the Meiji Restoration in Japan was such an example— and what Roosevelt did with the New Deal; so people have to just understand that such a dramatic change is absolutely possible today."*

LaRouche PAC has taken the responsibility to drive President Trump and the Congress into this action. But this is also the responsibility of all Americans that think of themselves as citizens: those who have been actively supporting the President, or supporting Sen. Bernie Sanders; those who supported no one, out of disgust at the manipulation, and continued manipulation of the election, but who have wanted a drastic change in the deindustrialization and Wall Street speculation policy ruling the country; those who know people killed, or made homeless and impoverished by Wall Street's induced "natural disasters." All must now act and make their voices heard.

Because, watching what is happening, again, to great American cities, leads anyone sane to the same conclusion: There is no alternative.

EIR**Contents**

www.larouchepub.com Volume 44, Number 36, September 8, 2017

Cover This Week

vanweezy.blogspot.com

MANHATTAN DIALOGUE

Hurricane Harvey Disaster Made by Wall Street

The following is an edited version of the dialogue which took place at the LaRouche PAC Manhattan Project meeting on Saturday, Sept. 2, 2017. Brian Lantz of the La-Rouche PAC Houston office was the special guest speaker.

Diane Sare: Good afternoon. I would like to welcome everyone here on this Labor Day weekend Saturday. As people are aware, Kesha Rogers, who is very well known around the country for having won two Democratic Party primaries for Congress in Texas and having come near winning the primary for U.S. Senate, was scheduled to be our speaker, but she is unable to be here because of a terrible tragedy that occurred as a result of this completely avoidable damage caused by Hurricane Harvey. As many of you know, but some may not know, her father and stepmother were swept off a bridge in their vehicle, and both perished on Wednesday. I would like to express our condolences to Kesha Rogers and her husband Ian Overton, her family, and everyone there who is dealing with this. The *New York Times* heard about this tragic accident and came to interview family members of her father, who was a local minister. Kesha was interviewed, and she said look, this is something that is affecting everyone; it's not just my family. People are suffering and they're suffering needlessly. So, even in this crisis, she is taking the kind of leadership that we know her for.

With us today will be Brian Lantz, from our Houston office, who will be giving a report on the situation and what can be done about it. As people are aware, the LaRouche Political Action Committee has put out a policy statement on this, which I think is long overdue and urgently needed.[1] I am very sorry to say that the pathetic state of mind of our members of Congress is

Air National Guard/staff Sgt. Daniel J. Martinez

An aerial view of extensive flooding in southeast Texas, Aug. 31, 2017.

---

1. See editorial in this issue

such that no one among them has thought to put out such a statement. The headline of *The Hamiltonian* newspaper this week carries that as the lead article: "Harvey Disaster Made by Wall Street! LaRouche Issues Emergency Plan of Action."

There are many crises in the nation which are catastrophes on the brink of occurring. Since the assassination of President Kennedy, and really since the Presidency of Franklin Roosevelt, we have been so negligent in making those investments and those leaps in scientific progress that would allow us to be able to address "natural disasters," weather conditions and so on before they occur. The city of Houston is far more populous than it was in 1948, at about the time the last dams and levees were built. Similarly, as people know, we discussed here a week ago the New York City transportation system. Penn Station was built for 250,000 people; it now carries 650,000, and it hasn't been upgraded. You don't have to be a genius to recognize that if a system is built for a certain number of people and you put triple or quadruple the number of people there and you make no changes or adjustments in that, that something is going to give way.

That's the point that we are making—that this catastrophe, including the tragic death of Kesha's father and stepmother, did not have to occur. I think really each of us should take those precious lives and the lives of others who have been lost in this, as a sacred trust that we will insure that no one ever dies in such a fashion ever again; that our nation is going to transform—to join the civilized world, which is right now led by China and Russia, and we are the ones who are going to have to make it happen, because particularly the Congress has been completely absurd in their response. I received an email this morning from the wife of Phil Murphy, who's running for governor of New Jersey. You'd think that someone running for office in New Jersey, which was devastated by Hurricane Sandy, might have something future-oriented and important to say about what's happening in Texas. Her letter was simply saying we are in solidarity with Houston; people helped us, so now you should donate to the Red Cross. Nothing of the nature of what is actually required.

Brian will have a lot more. I just want to now give you a little bit of a sense of where in the world we are and where all of this is occurring. First of all, I think everyone should remember and always have in the back of your mind, that until Glass-Steagall and Lyndon LaRouche's Four Laws are acted upon in the United States and in the trans-Atlantic system, we are facing a spec-tacular blow-out of the banking systems of the United States and Western Europe. More and more is occurring on this on a daily basis, and it's fueling a kind of desperation and insanity in some of these decisions, which underscores this.

I watched this morning a very beautiful four-minute video about Port au Prince in Haiti. China is going to invest $4 billion in the development of this city. I was thinking, China has built a lot of new cities in the last period, so this is not a new thing for them. It's very well thought out; it is phenomenal. The video goes through—because this is another area prone to flooding—all of the systems that are going to be built in the re-construction of the city to deal with massive flooding, to insure that transportation is unaffected by this; that communications are not affected by this; that they are building a water treatment plant that can process 225,000 cubic meters per day, or something close to that, if they have such an emergency. It is beautiful, and I think you have to ask yourself—and this gets back to this Wall Street question—if Haiti and Chad now with the Transaqua project in the middle of Africa, if these places can collaborate with China to build massive water management projects and modern new cities—we have to ask what is wrong with us? Why are people not even demanding this?

The last thing I'll just say is what we've seen, as we saw on September 11th, and what we've seen around hurricane Harvey—there is a spirit of the American people, a spirit of generosity, a spirit of self-sacrifice, a spirit where people absolutely come together in a crisis. All of the nonsense that the FBI and George Soros were trying to release after the staged Charlottesville events, has now been submerged under about twenty feet of water and we have now a potential. I think we have to take this moment of this storm and the tragedy that occurred with Kesha's father and stepmother,—probably the death toll is going to rise as they're able to get to more people and discover the damage—and say "OK. We will take this to pull our nation together." This is the inclination of the American people in their better selves. Lyndon LaRouche has been putting forward the program for this for forty years. Had then FBI Director Robert Mueller not led a witch hunt against Lyndon LaRouche in the '80s when LaRouche had been working with President Ronald Reagan; had LaRouche been allowed to become the President of the United States, you can imagine what the United States would look like today. We have an image of that, because the projects that Lyndon LaRouche has been fighting for for the last 40 years—the Kra Canal, the Transaqua project, and

others—are now being built, and we can do this here in the United States.

With that being said, I will turn this over to Brian Lantz from our Houston office.

Brian Lantz: Good afternoon. Thank you, Diane. It's good to be with our friends there in New York. This is both a solemn moment, but also one of real potential; a cause of real optimism. We saw this last week as we were being inundated. We saw photos sent down to us from the field organizing teams up there, including near Rockefeller Center, with these giant signs—"Houston: We Have a Solution!" You can imagine that this was sent out widely around here, circulated. And LaRouche's Four Laws, of course, are that solution. Kesha Rogers suggested that I stand in for her; and I'm going to do that here today. Certainly, I will be glad to take your questions. Another addition, in terms of New York—I believe the first emergency help that we had, emergency volunteers coming in to the greater Houston area, were from the New York Fire Department; certainly they were among the first. I think that's definitely worth mentioning here right off the bat.

The Storm and the Response

This is an enormous, unfolding crisis. I'm going to try to take you through some of this. I want to emphasize this is a blow to the whole country, to the world. This is not something to be taken as something just happening here. We certainly don't look at it that way ourselves. But, this is still unfolding. At last report we have 130,000 homes surrounding Houston that are on boiling water notice; that's 130,000 homes, and that's probably an understatement. That's just what's known to the state agencies at this point. Beaumont—1.5 to 2 hours to the east of us down Interstate 10—is underwater. They've been evacuating the evacuation centers because the waters are still rising from the Neches River. Port Arthur: this is still unfolding right now. Rescue operations are continuing; it's not over.

Waters are rising, including here in Houston, in the bayous. Buffalo Bayou, which runs through the city of Houston, is still slowly rising because water has to be released—controlled releases—from the Atticks Reservoir and the Barker Reservoir, which are within the Houston city limits, but also over the emergency spillway at Atticks. We'll come back to that later. That water has got to go into the Buffalo Bayou, and it's got to go down that bayou to reach the Gulf ultimately. This is striking everyone. The Buffalo Bayou flows through the Memorial City area, some of the nice areas shall we say, of the city, and they're underwater. Just yesterday, Mayor Sylvester Turner ordered further evacuations out of that area because of the rising waters, and because resources are stretched; manpower is stretched. I think those are just a few elements, and we'll come back a little more to the physical economy of this in a minute.

There's been a tremendous outpouring of aid, of help, of person-to-person effort made in the course of this unfolding disaster. I'm sure you've heard some about it, so I'm not going to belabor it; but we've had the Cajun Navy in here from Louisiana—a large, informal ad-hoc volunteer group of private boat owners who assist in flood search and rescue efforts. This is hundreds and hundreds of men and women with their boats and their high-rise vehicles towing their boats—coming in here, getting as close as they can into Houston; but now also into Port Arthur and Beaumont which is right there on the Louisiana border. Portions of Louisiana have been hit over the last few days as well, as the storm moved north to Louisiana, Arkansas, and Tennessee. Hundreds and hundreds of volunteers, at the request of law enforcement agencies, the mayor, the state, came in. This is going on up and down the coast.

If we go to the slides there, the first one [**Figure 1**] is a picture of downtown Houston, taken a few days ago. It just gives you a quick snapshot impression;

you've seen others, I'm sure, in the media. [**Figure 2**] is a scene I believe that was taken by LaRouche PAC member Peter Bowen the other day. This is what's going on in terms of the recovery effort. People are back to their homes; they're trying to tear out the sheet rock, get the carpet out. They're trying to rescue their homes. A matter of days underwater, and a house just quickly begins deteriorating. Mold and so forth, but also just physical deterioration. If you look down the street, you can see that at house after house after house, this is going on, even at the same time that rescues are still going on elsewhere; particularly in the perimeter now increasingly of Houston proper.

The next slide [**Figure 3**] is from one of the evacuation centers. We have somewhere on the order of 30,000 (and counting) people in evacuation centers to just get water, food, a dry place to sleep for their families, for themselves. Most people don't want to be in an evacuation center; you can't do anything for your house, you can't do anything for your neighbor, you can't do anything for your extended family, while you are sitting in an evacuation center. So, these are desperate circumstances. The numbers in these centers are beginning to drop now; at least in the Houston area. Beaumont, Port Arthur is another question.

To step back, I think the next slide [**Figure 4**] is of Hurricane Harvey coming onshore. That was a week and a day ago, in Rockport, a small commercial and sports fishing town that was completely wiped out. It's near Corpus Christi, quite a ways down the coast. But as you see, the outer bands of that storm to the east, to the right of that picture; those bands were coming in more or less simultaneously with the arrival of the storm, the direct hit in Rockport itself. Those bands are carrying the massive amounts of water that came in, roughly from 30 to 50 inches. Something on the order of 9-10 trillion gallons of water fell as a result of Hurricane Harvey over

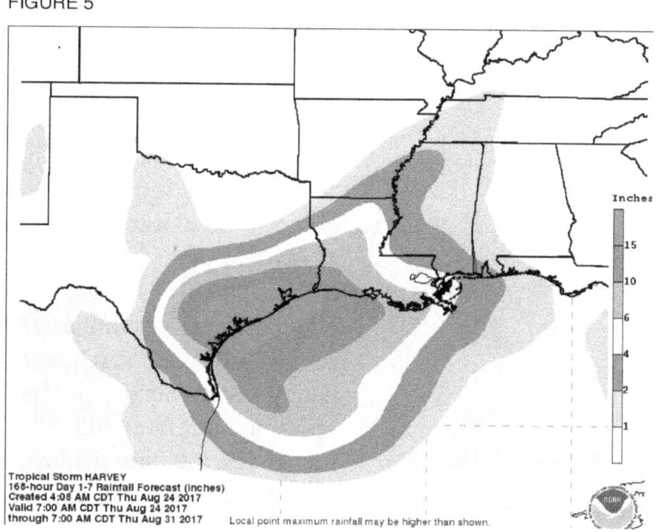

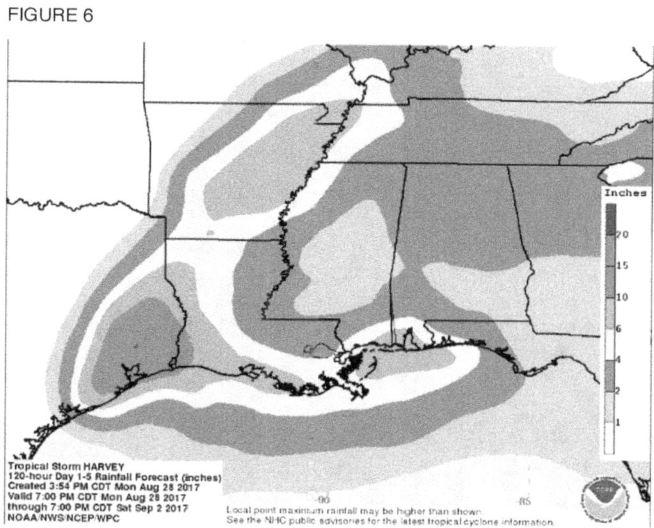

this large area, stretching from Corpus Christi up to Beaumont, Port Arthur, and beyond over to Lake Charles in Louisiana. [**Figure 5**] gives you a picture of the storm and again, a sense of that radiating impact. Note the gauge on the right; this was only forecast as it was coming onshore. The top of the gauge is 15 inches. [**Figure 6**] is, as the storm moves farther out. You see the rain gauge. Of course, it went way beyond that as well. That gives you a running sense of this thing.

On President Trump, I think it's important to say, that compared to what we saw with Obama, where he turned a cold shoulder to Haiti, despite proposals from the Army Corps, from the Joint Chiefs, and from the LaRouche organization, for a massive mobilization in the aftermath of the 2010 earthquake—nothing was done from the top down. Instead all you had was NGOs and self-help, and the Clinton Foundation and so forth. The point is, Haiti is now *worse off* than it was before that earthquake, certainly from before. Think also of Bush and Hurricane Katrina in 2005.

Compared to that, there's been a mobilization. There are something like 12,000 National Guardsmen active, most from Texas, but also coming in; that number will probably peak at around 24,000, according to Governor Abbott. There are also approximately 12,000 members and officials from FEMA, and they're already beginning to cut checks that simply help people pay for hotel rooms and food. This is just the beginning. There are also Coast Guard and police—we've seen hundreds and hundreds of police come in in vehicles from around the country, really as brigades to relieve offi-cers here, men and women who haven't slept in days.

There has been a lot of pre-positioning of resources, a lot of deployment of resources; getting people into evacuation centers, getting them water, food, and related emergency needs. All of that has been ongoing.

Economic Devastation

On the physical economy side of this, this is obviously not just a human tragedy, this is a body blow. I want to mention right off, agriculture. Thirteen or more of the fifty counties directly affected in Texas are agricultural; they're cotton producers, and those bales of lint, of raw cotton, are now ruined. The storage facilities they were in, the roofs were blown off. You can just imagine the extent: the rice crop and so forth, all of these things are affected, affecting farmers, ranchers, and their families.

Now we get to oil and gas. Colonial Pipeline, as we've mentioned over the past couple of days, is *the* major pipeline in the United States. It stretches from the Houston refineries, taking in fuel from as far away as Lake Charles; it takes it all the way right up to Atlanta, Washington, D.C., and also to the Port of New York. That pipeline is shut down. It normally carries diesel fuel, jet fuel, and gas. This complex of pipelines is now all shut down. They're hoping to have it opened up by the end of this weekend, but this is 20%, maybe 30% of U.S. refining capacity that is currently shut down, with major ramifications for the economy. That's worth bringing into the picture.

The port facilities: The next slide is a simple map

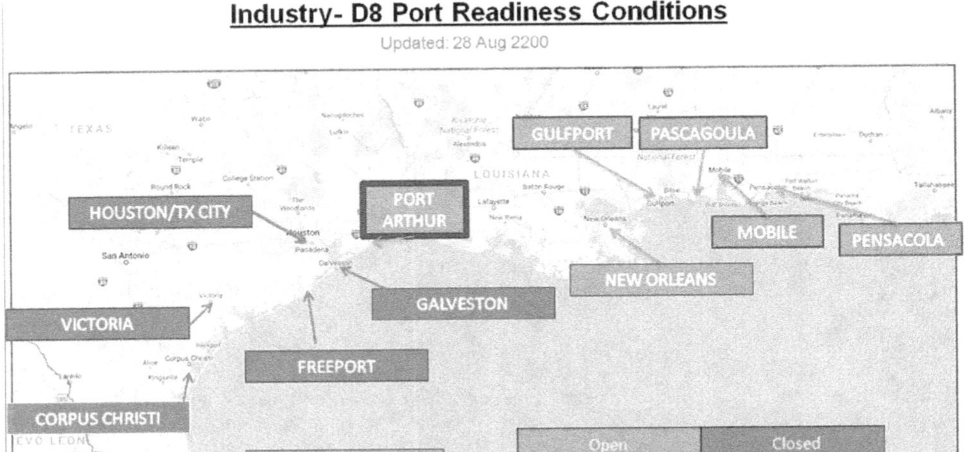

marking out the ports along the Third Coast [**Figure 7**]. That's the Gulf Coast, nicknamed "the Third Coast," which is 930 miles long, from Florida around to Harlingen and Brownsville and the Mexican border in the South.

Eight out of the 12 largest ports in the United States, by tonnage, are on that coast, from Mobile, Alabama on around to the West. We're talking about Beaumont and Port Arthur. Port Arthur is now closed, and shown in red, as all of the closed ports are. Houston is the second largest port. The largest is in Louisiana, the South Louisiana port between Baton Rouge and New Orleans. On around to Corpus Christi are smaller ports, including the barge port of Port Victoria, a city of 65,000 people. It's now on boiling water notice. Beaumont lost their water system. They can't get to it to repair it because it's under water, both of its major components, so obviously, people have got to get out because there's no water—period. No water. This port complex, and its tonnage and its role in the U.S. economy, is a very important and staggering dimension that Hurricane Harvey brings into focus.

The Port of Houston, the second largest port, is still closed down. It's opened for truck traffic now, but the port itself is shut. The San Jacinto-Brazos Basin drains into the ship canal and otherwise into the Galveston Bay, from the northern end of that inlet of water, a man-made connection. That stream of water is now carrying debris, it's carrying silt; the storm itself produced a 15-foot surge—nothing like Hurricane Ike that produced a 38-foot surge, but nonetheless, there's a question of whether, and how soon, ships can get back in there to deliver cargo or take cargo out. The Army Corps of Engineers has to go in there. Emergency dredging may be required. Debris has got to be cleared. The current is another factor. This is ongoing.

The oil refineries are going to be closed, probably at least in part, for weeks to come. All this is the consequence, as we've emphasized in the LaRouche PAC emergency statement, of not building, maintaining, and improving the nation's infrastructure and training and deploying a qualified workforce that goes with it. This is another body blow to our immune system, that's been contunually weakened ever since the death of Franklin Delano Roosevelt in 1945. Lyndon LaRouche's Four Laws—Glass-Steagall, national banking and National Bank, to issue national credit, and a science-driver program around fusion energy—is the only way this can be solved, top down.

In regard to the port and the trucking end of things, the getting in and out of the port is a problem in and of itself. A lot of highways are still shut down at various points. Sections of railroad track are under water. Texas has 10,000 miles of freight railroad track. more than any other state. But if you can't get in and out of the ports, because the rail lines were built on low-lying land in the first place, now you pay a multiple of what you thought you saved before. And the port's containers, all that's shifted in the course of the storm, and there's all the muck to be cleaned out. Again, this is going to be an ongoing process.

Science versus Irrationality

What I want to do at this point is to proceed and look at this from the standpoint of the engineering, a little bit of the science, but mostly the engineering—in terms of the infrastructure of this situation and perhaps put it under a microscope.

First of all, when you take into account the whole coastline that you saw in the course of those last few slides—the Gulf Coast coastline is all littoral, it's all low lying. The lay of the land has to be kept in mind. It's not something that can just be walked away from, it's something that has to be approached rigorously and scientifically—again, from the top. It's a vast flood-plain, is another way of putting it. The *highest point* in Houston is fifty feet above sea level; so for example, a dam that you build in Houston is not the Oroville Dam up there in Northern California. Lake Conroe reservoir in Texas that holds about 14% of what is behind the Oroville Dam, because there's no canyon behind Lake Conroe; it just spreads out. The capacity of dams is a major engineering issue in this area.

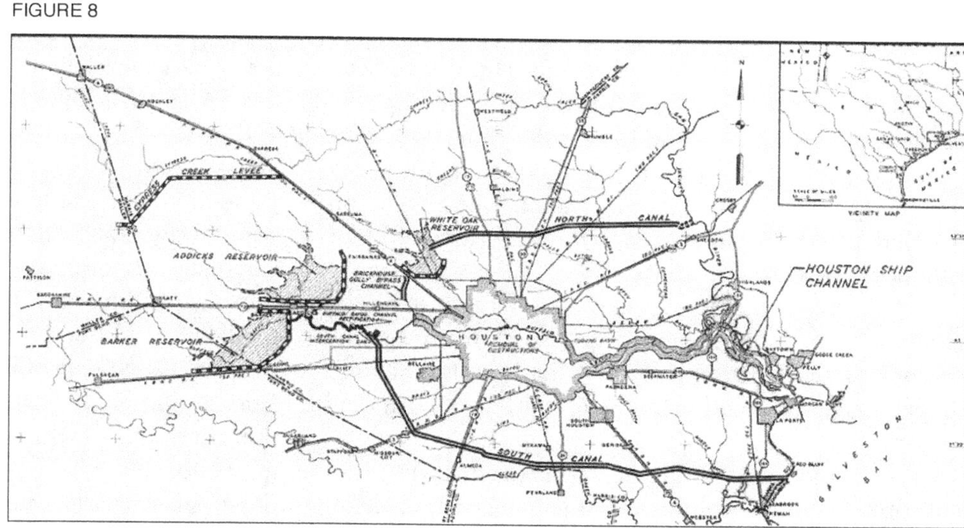

We've had only four Category 4 hurricanes hit the United States since 1970. In the thirty years prior to 1970, we had fourteen Category 4 storms, so this is not new. This is not a freak accident, which some people may think, or you may have read somewhere that Harvey was a 1,000-year storm. Dr. Roy Spencer is a noted meteorologist, Ph.D., who worked for NASA for decades, and is a top expert on weather. As Dr. Spencer points out we don't know if this is a "1,000 year storm," because we weren't around here 1,000 years ago. We weren't really around here 100 years ago, if you're talking about Houston—at least in terms of records, we weren't around here. Downtown Houston has seen higher water; back in December, 1935, it was 15 feet above what we saw with Hurricane Harvey. These are escape hatches, to escape not the water but to escape from responsibility, or more importantly from thinking through solutions; these have to be recognized as mirages.

On the other side, something you haven't heard about, is the South Texas Nuclear Project. This is right down there in Matagorda County, right down close to the water, not on the Gulf exactly, but it's right there on the Colorado River that runs through Texas (not the other Colorado River). There are two nuclear power plants in this facility; I believe it's the second largest in the United States. And Matagorda Bay is not far from Rockport and Corpus Christi; it was close to where Hurricane Harvey came ashore. This nuclear power station continued to operate right through Hurricane Harvey without a hitch. They had some advantages: They didn't need any fuel. They're halfway through their current cycles, they don't have to refuel until 2018. They didn't have any wet coal sitting out there being

drowned by Hurricane Harvey. They didn't have to wait for the sun to come out. And they had their team, about 250 men and women on site manning that facility, fully equipped, and they rode it out. I bring that up to inject the sense of optimism we rightfully should have, concerning our ability to master such crises, as opposed to getting the heebie-jeebies and running in the other direction, or simply falling into irrationality.

70 Years of Non-Development

How has this situation developed? **Figure 8** is a map of the Army Corps of Engineers project from 1940. That project resulted in the construction of two major dams. What you see, the total area there, that's now Houston; but you can see how small Houston was then, a few hundred thousand people in 1940 when this plan was drawn up. This is essentially the same system, minus some, that we have today. And there are some pluses. To the left you can see two crosshatched areas, which are the Barker and Addicks Dams. Farther around going clockwise, you can see a smaller one called the White Oak Reservoir, that was proposed but never built. The first two projects, Barker and Addicks dams were built, and those are the major dams on the Buffalo Bayou that have kept Houston itself from just completely drowning. Again, this is a flat, flood-plain area; Houston is laced with bayous. Houston's old nickname is the "Bayou City." This flood-plain geology and its bayous extends all along the coast from Louisiana and Mississippi through to Texas.

Barker Dam was finished in 1945 and Addicks in 1948. Those earthen dams, were labeled in 2009 as essentially in catastrophic condition, by the Army Corps of Engineers, which had built them and has maintained them as best they can with the resources they have been provided. Farther up to the left is the projected Cyprus Creek Levy. Around to the top on the right you see a canal labeled the North Canal, and down, again going to the right, you see a South Canal. They were all deemed a responsible approach by the Army Corps of Engineers way back in 1940.

There are no pumps in the system as it exists now. Houston doesn't have a pumping system in any significant way, and if you think about it, that's quite amazing, given Houston's location on the Gulf of Mexico and its history.

The Army Corps of Engineers can propose projects, but if the Congress doesn't pass them and if Presidents don't sign them into law, and if the American people don't demand them, they don't happen. They languish. And that's been the case here, as you can see from 1940. We didn't do then what was thought to be responsible. And now, the population of Houston is 2.2 million. The population of Harris County, which includes Houston, is 3.7 million. The larger region, which takes in six or seven counties, is an area larger than the State of New Jersey, just to give you some perspective on this.

But the Army Corps of Engineers operates from the standpoint that county Flood Control District staff work in conjunction with the State of Texas. They draw up plans, they propose how they're going to be built; they take these plans to the Army Corps. If they think they're competent, the Army Corps will sign off on them, and then it's up to these water authorities to then proceed, with the hope that Congress will then pass authorization to compensate the Districts for what they're building or want to build. This is the procedure as it exists today. The TVA would never have been built with this approach! Much of what exists across the United States—the Grand Coulee Dam, the Columbia River system, you name it—wouldn't be built under these conditions. The Federal appropriations coming in are what make these projects possible. I think that's a useful point to make.

Moving Toward Sanity

In terms of solutions, first of all, there is no dearth of hydrologists and specialists down here on water. There is the SSPEED Center—Storm Surge Prediction, Education, and Evacuation from Disasters—at Rice University. Texas A&M has a program. You may have heard of the "Ike Dike." After Hurricane Ike in 2008, there was an outcry, and visits were made to the Nether-lands and also specialists from the Netherlands came here. It resulted in the drawing up of what became known as "Ike Dike." There's a website http://www.tamug.edu/ikedike/. This was done in conjunction with Texas A&M University, to create a spine of sea surge protection barriers, man-made and otherwise, and then combining that with gates across the entrance into Galveston Bay, and on up into the ship canal that leads into Texas City, and then into Houston. This is minimally a $15 billion project.

That is one part of what rational people would consider a solution; it's part of what has been put in place in the aftermath of Hurricane Katrina, although as you may know, they have problems again there with breakdown of virtually every pumping station inside the bowl of New Orleans there—again, lack of foresight, to say the least. You have the Ike Dike, or something like it, but that's against storm surges; it's not a barrier against hurricanes.

Secondly, as you may already have thought of on reflection, Hurricane Harvey was a rain event. This is a hydrological event, more than a meteorological event in terms of just a hurricane and storm-surge. Thirty to fifty inches of rain falling in a matter of four or five days onto a flood-plain. That 1940 diagram shows some of what could have been done to move water. That South Canal would have moved water from the region of the Brazos River, which comes down the west side of the city, moved it on over and out into Galveston Bay.

The canal across the top, not so applicable to this immediate situation, would have brought water over to the San Jacinto. But, the San Jacinto is still overflowing—there are controlled releases—but the river is overflowing and drains into the ship canal and, so that canal is not so relevant to this immediate situation. That levy in the upper right-hand corner would have been a component. As spokesmen for the Army Corps of Engineers have said, if you widen the canals, you widen the capacity and the linkages among these bayous and the drainage systems and you can move a lot more water fast. And so, all are components of the required system.

Just to mention it, after decades of delay, the Luce Bayou Interbasin Transfer Project is moving forward. It will move water from the Trinity River, one of the half-dozen rivers running from north to south, east of the San Jacinto River system, over to Lake Houston, to increase the water supply for the city of Houston and all the surrounding bedroom communities and otherwise—surface water, because we don't want to draw

Courtesy of Chase Boogie

From drone footage of a flooded expressway in Houston, taken Aug. 27.

down the water here on the aquifers. That's a $5-6 billion project on the north side.

Another project—I just read an update on it in a Fort Bend publication—they're finally getting around to constructing the Allens Creek Reservoir project, which will be the biggest project on the Brazos River. You have flooding on the Brazos River, right now all the way up to close to Austin, from Bastrop on down. It's flooding now. Levees are breaking and being repaired; mass evacuations have occurred; mass flooding. These are large suburbs to the south of Houston proper.

The Brazos is flooding. These rivers and bayous are not going to be receding for weeks in many cases; the refineries closed for weeks—you get the idea.

Coming back to the Luce Bayou and Allens Creek projects, in the case of Trinity and San Jacinto, they're beginning to do inter-basin linking of water, to move water not only one way, but vice versa: to move it where it is needed and to move it out of where it's not needed. India is already doing this.

Because there's not much in the way of mountains in between, we could move water west to the Ogallala [or other] Aquifer over toward San Antonio and that region there. The Ogallala Aquifer stretches way north out of Texas—but it's been drawn down for decades, and needs to be recharged.

Hal Cooper, of Cooper Consulting, whom many of you know, pointed to plans dating back to in the early '60s, when John Connally was Texas Governor, to

move water from the Mississippi system all the way to the Ogallala Aquifer. We can build a system of reservoirs, running east-west, connecting them via pipelines and canals, to move water to the Ogallala Aquifer, or other aquifers, when needed.

Texas has a general water shortage. Before Hurricane Harvey arrived, we had drought conditions here in the South-Southwest and the Southeast, so there's much need for surface water here, so as note to draw down existing aquifers. Imagine a network of these systems running east-west and moving water between these basins. That's part of the direction we can go.

On the LaRouche PAC Webcast last night, Matt Ogden showed some of the photos of Tokyo's wonderful and massive underground system, the [Metropolitan Area Outer Underground Discharge Channel] that they have built. Tokyo is also essentially at sea level. We could do something like what Tokyo has done.

Question: Hi, it's Bruce from New Jersey. I have a background in construction. When I started working in the construction field in the '70s, what is now the Port of Elizabeth and Port of Newark, was swampland, which was built up by the dredging spoils that were brought onshore, built up the land area; and what was built there was huge shipping, transfer points, associated industries, all throughout that area. Looking at it now, you would never realize that from what was back in the '70s.

I think the major problem is not engineering or anything like that, it's the thinking of people within Congress. For example, Ted Cruz voted against the relief effort for Hurricane Sandy in New Jersey and New York. I have a lot of family in Florida, and congressmen there were voting against Sandy relief, and people were just astounded. There were letters to the editor in the papers, saying: "Are these people crazy? If they don't want to have the nation spend the money to help out people in New Jersey and New York—what happens when we get hit by a hurricane?" And really, that's what you're talking, in the case of Houston: There's no long-term thought on the question of whether it's infrastructure or whatever.

What was brought to my mind immediately was the vision of Kennedy dedicating a dam. I forget the exact name of the dam, but he was saying "this dam is here now, because people made the effort 20, 30 years ago, and that's what got us here today, and we've got to think about where we're going for the next 20 and 30 years." So you've really got to have the effort. There's more of a sense of the nation as a whole, versus this state's rights or "it's not my problem" kind of issue.

We have to redevelop that sense of the nation as a whole among people across the country, and particularly among legislators.

Lantz: As Helga Zepp-LaRouche has recently re-emphasized, why not build fifty new cities in the United States? And build them from 100, 200 feet underground going up, building in the kinds of systems needed for a population of a half-million to a million from the get-go. China's doing that.

It is a matter of looking from the future back to ourselves, and where we've gone awry. But let me also emphasize, this is a moment where we can move the country, not simply because of events here in Houston or the Gulf Coast, but because of events everywhere. The shocks are being delivered hard and fast, but there are also political shocks. We see it down here; you've got congressmen scrambling to fall into line. The *New York Times* had an article the other day on how suddenly the whole agenda going forth for the White House, as well as for Congress, is in flummox. The Republicans, including Ted Cruz, are now promoting massive Federal Funds for Hurricane Harvey relief, of course. A lot of these are Southern Republicans. But the point is, who's going to direct this to an effective solution? We've got some billionaires down here, including Michael Dell of Dell Computer, who are already offering tens of millions of dollars toward Hurricane Harvey relief, and we've got football stars and Hollywood stars—but this is what Haiti got! You had Hollywood stars over there in Haiti. And it didn't amount to a hill-o'-beans as we used to say.

So I agree absolutely, but we should really be clear: We have a moment here in our history, and a capacity, a potential to unite with other leading nations, led by China, to unite with the Belt and Road, that didn't exist ever before. And so we've got to go with this. Our emergency statement for emergency action. Absolutely, as Helga emphasized, Trump should declare an economic emergency for the nation. That's what's required: Let's cut through the tape. If we can reconstitute the Oroville Dam in a matter of a few months, at the orders of a greenie like California's Gov. Jerry Brown, we can move mountains.

Sare: I'd like to add something to that, which is our plan of action and the headline on the paper *The Hamiltonian*, "Harvey Disaster Made by Wall Street." I don't know if the $26 billion we've heard about would have covered all of the canals and the other projects that Brian showed, but it sounds like some aspect of that as he went through: this was $15 billion, that was $5 billion—$26 billion dollars.

Now, remember 2008: Remember the blowout of the insurance agencies that were insuring the mortgage-backed securities and the so-called housing bubble, and the system was about to blow. And it's a financial system! If that had been allowed to collapse, it would not have killed people. I know we were told by then Treasury Secretary Hank Paulson, that they were going to have to impose martial law if the markets were allowed to crash—but the markets are simply a construct of human beings. The money itself has no intrinsic value. Now, to prop up something which was illusory, they came up with *$700 billion dollars!* For nothing! For worse than nothing.

And then, I remember that Christmas, all of these crooks who should be in jail, who created this mess, were getting multimillion-dollar bonuses. And I think the most apt thing I read in some newspaper was from a barber in Connecticut who made the very apt analogy: He said, "You know, if I were cutting someone's hair and I accidentally chopped off a piece of their ear, I would not expect to get a tip! But the people who brought us this mess, got millions and millions of dollars in bonuses; and they're probably all being awarded professorships at major universities so they can teach other people how to rip us off." *This worship of money is insane!* It is totally artificial; it is manmade.

There's a scientific principle from our nation's founders involved here. Benjamin Franklin wrote on the subject of paper currency; Alexander Hamilton emphatically had a profound—the best—scientific understanding of this, of anyone prior to Lyndon LaRouche: The purpose of money is as an *instrument* to allow the development of human creativity. And the source of wealth is actually not anything you can put your hands on. The things that we see, whether it's dams or high-speed rail or spaceships—these are like the footprints of another process, which is the development of the human mind! This is how the human species transforms itself, that it is literally the case that we should be a different species than the human species that had no electricity or running water four or five generations ago. You want to create a society which fosters human potential to do that—and that's the measure of wealth, not money.

Everyone here should be calling your congressman and your senator, saying, "cut the crap, we don't need a war with Russia. You've been insane, so far. We need this emergency program, and you should work with President Trump to get this done." And you should get the statement that's on the LaRouche PAC website under the headline "No More Houstons." It's in *The Hamiltonian* under "Harvey Disaster Made by Wall Street" Congress should be bombarded by American saying, "I got your stupid email: You're telling us to give money now to the Red Cross. That's fine, I'm sure they need it, but where were you, when we needed $26 billion in flood control in Houston?" We just heard from Brian, that the Congress knew in 2009—eight years ago—that these levees were decrepit and dysfunctional. The Army Corps of Engineers told them so. We had *eight years*, and we did nothing?

But somehow we found $700 billion in 24 hours to bail out a bunch of crap! I think Neil Barofsky, who served as the Special Inspector General in charge of overseeing TARP from December 2008 until March 2011, said the total bail-out was *$23 trillion*! So we can find *$23 trillion* so that the people who were snorting cocaine can keep their day trading jobs on Wall Street, but we cannot find a fraction of that, to actually address what's going on in the nation!

Everyone has to take this very personally. Don't be intimidated, and don't take "No" for an answer: What happened in this country is completely unacceptable!

Question: It seems to me a paradigm unto itself that the scientists tell society what is needed and how to maintain it, and the bean counters, the management people, find a means and a way to jeopardize the systems that the people, the scientists have developed.

An example: My father was an electronic engineer for Bell Laboratories. He designed direct distance dialing (DDD) circuitry. In it, he had designed maintenance, which was almost automatic. At that time, we were still thinking economically in school, that "long term" was twenty-five years, and the "short term" was five years. Now the long term is maybe a year; and the short term is a few months.

It's the penny-wise, pound-foolish phenomenon: As soon as management has a say over what the scientists have developed over great research, they'll come up with something six bucks short. What can we do about that? This is endemic in this country. Why are we so backward? After Katrina they put in the sea gates, and some pumping systems—a little bit, not even everything that was needed! So you're talking about maybe $9 billion compared to the $130 billion loss in property and life (not that you could ever put money on a human life).

So it's the foolishness, the empty-mindedness of people saying, "well, according to my abacus, here, we can't afford this, but we'll put something else in."

Sare: I think that's very clear. I'll just say that Lyndon LaRouche has written paper upon paper about accountants, and why you would never have an accountant run a business. The accountant has a purpose, and LaRouche knew this because he did management consulting; he went into companies to find out what they were doing wrong, and why they were having trouble. One of the other things he said, is that whatever it is they tell you is going well, that's the first thing to check.

An accountant does have a purpose: to keep you out of jail. So there is something that is valid, but they should never, never be making policy direction decisions.

Lantz: I think we've covered the coastline so to speak, and more importantly we've covered what has to be done. Kesha Rogers sent in a message the other day: "Keep fighting." She wasn't speaking of rear-guard actions, she was speaking of driving for victory: It's within reach, we have the solutions. Let's get these ideas out there and recognize what's there to leverage, now.

GLASS-STEAGALL & BEYOND

Our Credit System

by Lyndon H. LaRouche, Jr.

*On mid-day, Wednesday, October 19th, during a full hour's span of the broadcast LPAC **Weekly Report**, my associates had joined in presenting the essential preconditions which were required to rescue both the U.S. republic, and also mankind more widely. We worked in the effort to rescue society from what has now become a virtually immediate threat of a massive wave of, virtually paleolithic "extinctions" against the presently crumbling, trans-Atlantic cultures of mankind. The report reported here presents certain among the most essential features of a wave of threatened Hitler-like "extinctions" now authored by such as U.S. President Barack Obama and his British royal accomplices, but it also points toward some urgently needed, hopeful remedies required to bring such bestiality as theirs to an end.*

As I shall identify that universal principle of science in this report, the human species has been distinguished from other species by what I have defined as *"an expression of physical science to be known as the principle of credit."* That notion is the most crucial, and also most hopeful option, but, therefore, also, for some persons, the most rejected of those conceptions on which the continued existence of the human species now depends for guidance. The unfortunate fact about that principle, is that the crucial elements of the practice of that particular knowledge had remained, largely, as being limited, heretofore, largely to my own knowledge of relevant types of physical-economic functions. This has been knowledge gathered, so far, during recent decades. Now, most recently, since my September 30th national broadcast, that knowledge has now begun to be spread somewhat more widely.

On the evening of September 30th , first, and then, in greater detail in the October 19th LaRouche-PAC "Weekly Report," the proverbial "ice" has finally broken publicly.

Among most people until now, much of this important knowledge had remained widely neglected. It had been knowledge which seemed to have been a kind of knowledge more or less easily avoided by most, even among those stubbornly careless persons who had been given adequate access to that knowledge, but had declined to master it. The result had been, that what had been put in jeopardy in that way, until now, had been *the same, actually indispensable universal physical principle*, the so-called "credit principle," which I identified, summarily, by the presentation of the set of a brief series of questions and answers delivered during my live national broadcast of September 30, 2011.

Since that September 30th broadcast, certain leading economists, and others of similar disposition, had reacted to that broadcast by announcing their recognition of this point of knowledge, after hearing the dialogue with which that report had concluded.

So, presently, a notable amount of relevant detail on this same subject, is now being included on the record, this time in the extended remarks on this same subject both by me and by some among my associates, as in the instance of the continuation of that national broadcast's theme now expressed in the already mentioned audio-visual "Weekly Report" of this past Wednesday, October 19th.

EIRNS/Stuart Lewis

In his Sept. 30 webcast, "An Emergency Presidential Address," Lyndon LaRouche "broke the ice" publicly, on the physical science known as the "principle of credit." He is shown here on that occasion.

On the one side of the experience of societies, it can be argued that that specifically human potential for a rigorously scientific definition of creativity, should already have become commonly accessible to relevant scientists. This is something which should have been known scientifically in such circles by virtue of consideration given to the uniqueness of an intelligent mankind's inherent nature. Despite such helpful developments as that would represent, the negligent error from the past still persists today among the large majority of relevant categories of professionals.

That needed correction should have been made by means of both the actually creative nature of the quality of the voluntary exercise of that discovery, and by the application of those universal principles of specifically human knowledge and action which are absent, categorically, among all other known varieties of living species. However, it often remains the case, that societies, and most of the individuals of which they are composed, still lack effective knowledge of that very principle which defines the domain of their naturally given creative potential.

So, even among many scientists, it may be often their inclination even to defy this evidence; they have often been even induced either to fear such branches of knowledge, or they simply evade such academically "troublesome" knowledge, because it is "not recog-nized as having been popular among the relatively ignorant." Often, such negligence has been spread under the influence of the dupes of Bertrand Russell's swindles who had been taken in—*"in droves!"*—by the radically reductionist swindles of the late 1920s Solvay conference. Or, for kindred reasons, some might even hate that capacity for actually creative willfulness on which the expression of human creativity depends, on which the presently continued survival of the cultures of the human species may have depended.

The subject which I have now introduced in this present location, and in this fashion, requires further, and broader clarification bearing on the essential, most principled features of the ancient through modern history of European civilization. I emphasize the fact, that the subject which we consider here, is not a mere matter of opinion. This is the subject of a rigorously scientific matter. It is no "mere matter of science;" it is also a matter on which the continued existence of a human civilization presently depends. It requires a rigorous study of the impact of that civilization's emergence and its effects on a much wider region and the deep future of our planet.

Therefore, those preliminary remarks uttered, I now proceed as follows:

I. The Americans vs. the Brutish Tyrants

The subject on which any and all competent consideration of national or global physical economy among nations absolutely depends at this time, is the notion of *a science of physical economy.*[1] That notion is an expression of the human power for deep insight which

---

1. Lyndon LaRouche, *Three Steps To Recovery?*, *EIR*, vol. 38, no. 40, October 14, 2011. Or, Lyndon LaRouche PAC (http://www.larouchepac.com/node/19759).

that science's root-expression combines with the characteristic features of the persistence and progress on which the human species depends otherwise. At the present instance, civilization finds itself trapped, that more or less desperately, at the brink of the global effects of a presently onrushing, general physical-economic breakdown-crisis of a virtually world-wide, British-imperialism-dominated system of oligarchical degeneracy, especially among the trans-Atlantic regions. Under present trans-Atlantic policy-shaping trends, we are between two days and a pair of weeks distant from a presently threatened, hyperinflationary breakdown-crisis in the trans-Atlantic financial systems: a hopeless breakdown now facing trans-Atlantic humanity at this present moment. Only a sudden and very radical shift to a strict Glass-Steagall policy could prevent such a general collapse of the trans-Atlantic region at this time.

Without at least a relatively primitive range of understanding of this matter so far, there could be no competent appreciation of the nature of, and the remedies for the deadly peril on which the rescue of the trans-Atlantic region (in particular) now depends.

In bringing that aforesaid, specific issue to bear respecting the principled features of the present trans-Atlantic plunge into a virtually terminal general breakdown-crisis of the entirety of British imperialism-dominated trans-Atlantic civilization, we, who possess the active intelligence required to understand the present world's economic-breakdown-crisis currently in progress, must proceed from *the foundations of a notion of the specific implications of a principle of creativity which I had introduced in Chapter I of my "Three Steps to Recovery."*

That notion is expressed as a principle to be conceived as being inherent in the distinction of a human principle of civilization, a principle unique to mankind among all other known species. It is to be fairly described as a principle which stands in opposition to the cultural characteristics of behavior of those actual human beings who are driven, like virtually human "cattle," into what is virtually a form of virtual captives cast in the roles of virtually dumb, British, or similar sorts of talking beasts.

This is a subject of those specific kinds of consciously creative powers of the human mind, the which are typified by the principles associated with the work of such pioneers in modern European civilization as the

EIRNS/Sylvia Rosas

Only a sudden and very radical shift to a strict Glass-Steagall policy could prevent a general collapse of the trans-Atlantic region at this time. Here, a LaRouchePAC organizer gathers signatures in support of Glass-Steagall, in San Diego, Calif.

great modern scientist Nicholas of Cusa and his followers, including such avowed followers of Cusa as both Leonardo da Vinci and Johannes Kepler. That latter pair from among the great minds of those times, typify great minds who have been widely defamed by the proponents of all those hateful varieties of oligarchical doctrines, such as those of the late Bertrand Russell, or, earlier, the notorious charlatan Adam Smith, whose offal-like intellectual product is mistakenly treated, even officially, for "science."

Thus, even scientific giants among the followers of Brunelleschi and Cusa, such as Leonardo da Vinci and Kepler, typify those forms of Classical expressions of culture, which have been hated by such as the late Bertrand Russell of "Cambridge systems analysis" notoriety. The modernist tradition of Russell, is that which has been spread by such dupes of Russell as the devotees of the International Institute for Applied Systems Analysis, "IIASA," and their likenesses, such as John v.

Neumann and Norbert Wiener.[2]

Some useful indications bearing on the lack of actual creativity (rather than mere innovations) within parts or entireties of some human cultures, or stratifications of "sub-cultures," are of the nature of errors located among actually well-known strata of ostensibly literate human cultures, including those from ancient through contemporary affairs. Those errors are to be located, chiefly, in instances of what are to be recognized as *oligarchical cultures.* Such is the legacy of ancient cultures of a series associated with that same *oligarchical principle* which is to be associated within a series of leading empires, beginning with such origins as that of ancient imperial Rome, as these expressions of perversity which have been

The Roman imperial forms of degenerate cultures, such that of the British monarchy of today, represent a type of oligarchical decadence, historically found in such empires as the Babylonian, Persian, Byzantine, and Venetian. Shown: From the five-painting series on "The Course of Empire," by Thomas Cole, the final stage: "Desolation" (1836).

continued through those decadent forms of neo-Roman imperialism met in the lurid instance of the Emperor Nero, or, among modern circles, the present-day British empire of Queen Elizabeth II today.

The specifically Roman imperial forms of degenerate cultures, such that of the British monarchy of today, or those cultures of the same elemental traits, represent a specific type of oligarchical decadence which is notable as being from among what are known to have been, or to be literate cultures. In the history of Mediterranean cultures, the notable types of oligarchical decadence are found in exemplary cases such as ruling systems such as those of the Babylonian heritage, of the Persian (Achaemenid) Empire, of the series of the Roman, Byzantine, and "Venetian-crusader" systems of imperialism, and of the modern British imperialism established through the agency of the New Venetian Empire of Paolo Sarpi and, later, Sarpi's follower, William of Orange.

The latter, the New Venetian empire of Sarpi follower William of Orange, is one typically represented by that original neo-Romantic maritime imperialism which was set into motion by such followers of Paolo Sarpi as William of Orange. Such is the origin of a modern British imperialism which was established as a British empire-in-fact, with the 1763 Peace of Paris; this was the same treaty which set into motion the beginnings, in 1763, of the rise of the British (or, better said, "brutish") imperial conquest of India.

To understand the strategic characteristics of the modern British empire's post-1763 origins in that "Seven Years War" which had concluded with that Peace of Paris, we must turn close attention to both the deeper and the more immediate roots of that continuing moral conflict between, on the one side, the British empire dated since that "Seven Years War," a war which is to be sharply contrasted, on the other, with the system of government and culture represented by the American Revolution's struggle against a shamelessly mass-murderously Romantic, British imperial tyranny which has been continued to the present day of the reign of Queen Elizabeth II.[3]

---

2. The form of overt British styles of evil expressed by Wiener, is to be found luridly displayed in Wiener's **The Human Use of Human Beings**.

3. The stipulated goal under current British royal family circles' policies, has been recently set at a hastened reduction of the human population to the order of one billion souls—a far, far greater slaughter than that of Adolf Hitler's regime.

That division requires us to emphasize the fact, that whereas, European nations and peoples have often revolted against the New-Venetian tyranny of the followers of Paolo Sarpi and his follower William of Orange, those same European nations have often submitted to that same British tyranny, and that, often, most importunely. Such is the case of that insanely mass-murderous British puppet, U.S. President Barack Obama.

Therefore, to understand the world system centered in the imperialism of the British empire of today, we require insight into a far deeper realm than were usually considered the root of this history of the trans-Atlantic conflict situated, principally in the domain of the North Atlantic.

That is the conflict which has been the source of the strife between the (predominately) patriotic current of the American revolution against the British imperialism of the followers of systemic irrationalism of a Paolo Sarpi. That British irrationalism persists, still today, through the followers of that rabid irrationalist, Adam Smith, who explicitly denied the existence of any semblance of rational beliefs among his duped believers. He and his dupes have continued their foolishness up to the present day of the lunatic, conventional practice of statistical forecasting methods. It is the persisting credulity of those dupes which has done much to make possible the ruinous continued existence of a British empire into the present modern times.

To define the category within which the European maritime-based civilization and its internal, now trans-Atlantic strife, are to be principally located, we must focus attention on the implications of the flight of the descendants of Europe into North America since the time of the exoduses of such as the Seventeenth-century Mayflower compact and that system of credit introduced to the Massachusetts Bay Colony of the Win-

The development of the American economy was based on the systems of integrated rivers and canals under Charlemagne, which provided the model for the development of the territory of North America under the same methods. This portrait of Charlemagne is by Albrecht Dürer (c. 1512).

throps and Mathers, which has laid the foundations for the central principle of the founding of the U.S. Federal Constitution.

Such are the essentials of an introduction to those underlying principles of a modern practice of physical science on which any competent expression of economic science depends.

II. The Credit Principle

Excepting the remarkable reforms of Charlemagne made in his time, there is no significant medieval indication of an effective insight into the principles of a practiced ancient or medieval economic science, other than that of the explicitly stated, leading features of Charlemagne's leadership on this account during those past times.[4] The nearest approach to a competently defined, modern form of political science, is located in the implications of the work of the Renaissance's Nicholas of Cusa;[5] the first blush of a competent form of a modern era's economic science, is to be located in the period of the great credit-system reforms of the independent Massachusetts Bay Colony under the leaderships of the Winthrops and the Mathers.

The physical-economic development of the productive powers of labor in what was developed to become the original United States, is to be located in the heyday of the Massachusetts Bay Colony, that under the Seventeenth-century reign of the interval under a sovereign form of that colony. Notably, the system of the development of the American economy before and during the founding and development of the United States, had

---

4. It were proper to qualify that by stating that this holds generally for times subsequent to the life of Plato, and, also, implicitly, Eratosthenes.
5. E.g., **De Docta Ignoratia**.

been based on such crucially significant means as that of the development of systems of integrated rivers and canals under Charlemagne; that development under Charlemagne, was the model for the development of the territory of North America under the same methods of rivers, canals, and a trans-continental American economy (e.g., transcontinental rail) copied from the precedents of Charlemagne's reign in the territories typified by the commonality roughly represented by the territory of France and Germany presently.[6]

In the competent notion of a science of economy, the active agent is not money, nor the exchange of money as such. It is to be located in the increase of the physical-economic growth of the "energy-flux density," per-capita and per-square-kilometer's measure of the increase of the physically productive expressions of the creative powers of human labor.

That much said along those lines this far, we are situated in the implacable conflict between the principle of the republic and that of the empires. Speaking in physical, rather than mere political terminologies, the most competent choice of a technical name for "imperialism," is that "oligarchical principle" based on the rule of society by the notion of "money as such," as expressed by the essential principle of action typified by the infamous Olympian motives of the exemplary Peloponnesian wars.

That much said, now go directly to the heart of the matter: *The Credit Principle* as I presented the essence of that matter, briefly in the question-and-answer epilogue to my September 30, 2011, LPAC National television broadcast.[7]

---

6. Indeed, the division of the territory of France from Germany, which occurred, originally, following the death of Charlemagne, became the means for organizing those conflicts within the territory of Europe through which the rebirths of the old Roman Empire were established in medieval and modern Europe up to the present day. In his later years, France's Fifth Republic President Charles de Gaulle expressed his acquired insight into the importance of establishing an anti-British-imperialist Europe from the Atlantic to the Urals, as my wife, Helga, and I, conspired with others in such an attempt during the period following the "Fall of the Wall." The development of technology has already created the preconditions, today, under which wars among nations are an enterprise in criminalizing insanity, as we have seen in the cases of the policies of the series of Anglo-American and related, medieval-like warfares since the assassinations of U.S. President John F. Kennedy and his brother Robert. The great strategic struggles of mankind are to be found within, and beyond the borders of our Solar System and that galaxy which contains the origins of our weather systems.

7. For background, turn to the thesis of my cited *Three Steps to Recovery*, Chapter I. "The Human Principle."

The Principle of Human Progress

The evidence of the functional difference of man from beast, is to be recognized in the evidence of the effects of science-driven, willful human physical-economic progress. That, in turn, depends upon the condition that this represents a net progress in mankind's power to exist at rates which outrun forms of depletion inherent in the function of attributable physical time.

This power, which is unique to the human species, is expressed in the most typical fashion as the increase of the power of the human individual and in his environment as measured fairly in both *relative capital-intensity of modes of production*, and in the relationship of the development of "basic economic infrastructure" to *relatively higher intensities of energy-flux density* as expressed *per capita*, by *the relative rates of increase of the human population*, by the *relative longevity of the population*, and by *the effectively applied relative productivity per capita.*

That set of points is illustrated most conveniently in the following modality.

The power of the human species to exist, depends on effects which are illustrated by the increase of *energy-flux density per capita and per square kilometer.* Those advances in the condition of the human individual, are fairly described in estimates, as being dependent upon the increase of the productive physical powers of labor, and upon related functions, per capita and per square kilometer. In other words, the continued existence of the human species depends upon an effective increase of the applied energy-flux density of power above and beyond the factor attributable to "the friction" of entropic tendencies.

The significance of that requirement, lies in the role of the quality of science-driven progress attributable to the development of the creative powers of the human mind, as this is fairly illustrated by the case of *the increase of effective energy-flux density achieved through the quality of the fundamental physical advances in that energy-flux density*, as this process is typified by leaps upward in *scientific creativity per capita and per square kilometer of territory.*

On that account, we must take into account what is fairly identified as the principle of evil which is attributable to that mythical Olympian Zeus who is otherwise identified as the expression of the evil, oligarchical principles of "zero growth," "low technology", and "population-size control." Think of the mythical Olympian Zeus, and of the actual British empire of today, as each is equivalent to being a virtual "Satan."[8]

It must be emphasized here, that the oligarchical

principle, on which the secular dogmas of the British monarchy's population-control doctrines are premised, is precisely such a pro-Satanic, Nietzsche-like oligarchical notion, a notion which is premised, today, as by the British oligarchical doctrine of the Adolf Hitler-like, mass-murderous population-reduction dogma of Britain's Schellnhuber, and, similarly, President Barack Obama's own evil doctrine.[9]

III. Science & the Credit System

All actually competent varieties of economic forecasts, on which I enjoy a relative monopoly so far in these times, have been consistently proven by me to have been (scientifically and systemically) competent. "Scientifically and systemically," as used, thus, as terms used by me here, are not mere descriptions, no mere hyperbole; they are absolutely physical-scientific terms employed by me to indicate "a matter of universal, physical-scientific principle."

I explain, as follows. The point I have just stated may be approached for explanations in a variety of choices of sequences of description; however, whatever the ordering of the terms of the argument, the outcome is approximately the same in effect, one, perhaps, preferred over the other, as a matter of intellectual taste. The outcome of any of those approaches is the initiate's encounter with a universal physical principle which most actually mentionable professionals in the domain of economic studies had never imagined before. However, happily, it has been recently demonstrated, that actually leading economists, as measured in performances, are often capable of discovering that principle, even almost immediately.[10]

It is perfectible admissible to identify the most typical failures of even most leading performers among economists, until most recently, as representing "a presently timely blunder of 'belief in the follies of Laplaceianism'." The same point may be identified as being a principle of human life which is not presently known to occur in any other known living species than mankind. In short, "it is time for mankind to grow up," would-be so-called "economists" most particularly.

The crucial evidence which defines the scientific, rather than the, unfortunately, presently still popular, mistaken "meaning" of "time," is located essentially in the practiced discovery of universal physical principles which mark the "clock-work like" transition of principles of human behavior associated with the generation-to-generation succession of mankind's progress through fresh discoveries of universal physical principles. I mean, especially, that succession in scientific pro.gress which began, predominantly, with the series of crucial modern discoveries in physical science which began with, and explicitly followed the precedents supplied in modern science since the pioneering work of the Renaissance which is signalled by the discoveries of Filippo Brunelleschi and Nicholas of Cusa. It has been the latter's achievements whose uniquely original discoveries included the great wave of modern transcontinental navigations.

---

8. Compare this with the denunciation of Aristotle by the Philo of Alexandria who was the friend of the Christian Saint Peter. Aristotle is described by Philo, implicitly, as the Satanic image of the modern Friedrich Nietzsche, and as the mother of the cults of both Euclid and Zeus. Aristotle's god was, like Nietzsche's, the prophet of the satanic religious belief of "God is dead." Euclid, for example, like Aristotle, proclaimed the "God is dead" doctrine, in effect. He argued, thus, that once the Creator had generated a universe, that the universe would be described as completed, and therefore incapable of any further creating. It was such a pro-Satanic doctrine, which has been derived from the oligarchical dogma of the Olympian Zeus, *et al.*, which had persisted in such expressions as the *apriorism* fraud of Euclidean geometry. A story within the story of **The Brothers Karamazov**, suggests a similarly pro-Satanic argument.

9. It is notable, that Bertrand Russell, writing in 1951, was a leading proponent of the genocide currently demanded by the British monarchy's asset Hans Joachim Schellnhuber, who has been a rabid proponent of the British royal circles' proposal to reduce the Earth's human population most suddenly and most radically, to no more than one billion wretched folk. Russell wrote: "... War, so far, has had no very great effect on this increase [of population], which continued through each of the world wars ... but, perhaps bacteriological war may prove more effective. If a Black Death could spread throughout the world once in every generation, survivors could procreate freely without making the world too full ... The state of affairs might be somewhat unpleasant, but what of it? Really high-minded people are indifferent to happiness, especially other peoples' ..." [Excerpted from a book planned and commissioned by me: Carol White, **The New Dark Ages Conspiracy**, 1980]. That Bertrand Russell dogma, is the dogma of the so-called "environmentalist movement" supported by the British royal family's household circles of the World Wildlife Fund still today.

10. Lyndon H. LaRouche, Jr., "LaRouche Emergency Address: Trans-Pacific Alliance Can Re-Launch Bankrupt Economy," *EIR*, October 7, 2011; [transcript of LaRouche LPAC-TV National Address delivered Sept. 30, 2011 or see Lyndon LaRouche PAC Also, LPAC *Weekly Report,* Oct. 19, 2011]

The greatest enemy of mankind known to us today, is that of the legacy of the "oligarchical principle," centered today in the British Empire, since the occupation of the British Isles by the mass-murderous predator known as William of Orange. Painting by Peter Lely (c. 1680-1720).

The Evil Traitors to Mankind

There is a certain leading source of complexities in that picture of history. To wit: the history of mankind and its cultures has been often held back, even nearly destroyed by the evil of the oligarchical systems, as in the case of the opposition to Plato (e.g., the legend of Prometheus), an opposition expressed by the evil influence of such as the figure of the Olympian Zeus and the evil of Aristotle's sundry varieties of deadly poisons. It is the intellectually and morally retarded behaviors of the nations and populations corrupted by the oligarchical cultures and their trends, which has embodied the force of those human evils, such as that of the current Queen of England and her lackeys, such as Barack Obama, which have underlain the influence of the oligarchical cultures such as those from ancient Rome through the present-day empires.

It will be most helpful, at this stage of our present report, to provide a convenient summary of the natural precedent for the rise and fall of attempted advances in the conditions of life of (either living or once) living species, that in order that we might refute that lying farce called the Nineteenth Century introduction of that blatant fraud known as "The Second Law of Thermodynamics."

I summarize that latter point, briefly, as follows.

The existence of known types of living species during a span of archeological investigations, since such as approximately a half-billion years ago, shows a leading trend in such heritages which shows life on Earth as steered in an upward train of increasing energy-flux density which has culminated in the combined biologies and biological potentials for actually expressed human mental life which defines the planet as naturally impelled to successively more powerful forms of life, especially human life, as so expressed for human progress in rising rates of energy-flux densities of human life per capita and per square kilometer of territory. It is that characteristic of human life, as distinct from all other known living species, which demonstrates mankind's inherently potential destiny now in mankind's leap into a leading role in extra-terrestrial human development of man's rising role, in not only the reach of our Solar system, but also, our rising practical influence into the galaxy which our Solar system inhabits.

Thus, the actual history which is natural to the human species, as opposed to the effects produced by the inherent depravity of the oligarchical systems such as those of the fabled, oligarchical Olympian Zeus, is to be traced along a pathway of defiant development, against the oligarchical principles of such as the Roman and British empires. The natural inclination of the human species, is of increased population and per-capita power of existence, all, so far, in defiance against the oligarchical depravity of many leading cultures of mankind.

Witness, for example, the inherent depravity of those socialized cultures which not mere hold back, but demand a reversal of human culture, setting mankind back, as the specifically ungodly, oligarchical characteristics of today's morally and physically degenerating and pro-mass-murderous do, such as those of the British monarchy and President Barack Obama.

That moral, and actually biological degeneracy of such as the so-called "modernists" presently, such as British puppet Barack Obama, is the true epitome of manifest evil. My point here, on that account of scientific matters, is that there is no "natural depravity" like that expressed by the current British monarchy, but only the malicious decadence inherent in that oligarchical principle's modern expression of the reign of the British empire spawned by the likes of the New Venetian Party's William of Orange and the followers of the virtual founder of contemporary global imperialism, Lord Shelburne, since that time. One may freely throw wretches such as England's monstrous Henry VIII and Paolo Sarpi's heritage of the New Venetian Party into the same rubbish-bin of lost cultural moralities which have served as instruments of scientific backwardness in the times of the history known to us presently from the past to present times.

All notable, and known general backwardness in human progress as such, has been the fruit of sheer evils such as those of the societies ordered in coincidence with the oligarchical principle. Once that point is adequately presented, the most important of the failures which have occurred within the powers of mankind, have been made clear. No other source of backwardness and related evils is to be blamed on an alleged lack of human natural qualities.

What confronts human society with its great shame, is nothing other than that evil, known as "the oligarchical principle," which, having once captured, seduced, and degraded naturally human beings, has been a state of affairs in which the early captors of relatively ignorant human populations, has held them in a captivity like that in which African slaves were held captive, not only in the Americas, but Africans taken into captivity, also by Africans prior to their captivity in the Americas, and Americans who are still kept largely within the effects of a slave-system among most of the current population of the Americas generally still today. The votes cast for U.S. Presidents such as the pathetic George W. Bush, Jr., and the luridly pro-Satanic British royal puppet, Barack Obama, illustrate that oligarchical tradition which has held most of the human population of our planet in virtual intellectual-cultural servitude, such as that typified by the inherent moral depravity of what was expressed by the 1950 launching of that Congress for Cultural Freedom which supplied the monstrous wave of immorality regnant throughout Europe since (and also actually before that time).

The greatest enemy of mankind known to us today, is that of the legacy of the same "oligarchical principle" currently centered in the British empire today since the murderous occupation of the British Isles under the flag of the same legacy of Paolo Sarpi expressed in the invasion of the Netherlands and the British Isles as the New Venetian party of the mass-murderous predator known as William of Orange.

Beyond the Oligarchies

All major warfare presently known to us concerning our historical knowledge of warfare on this planet, has been a product of either the "infectious disease-like" practice of warfare, or the necessary resistance to the oligarchical evil's extensive periods of reign upon relatively large regions of habitation. The practice of cannibalism, or its likeness, is the characteristic of a part of the human species whose policies and practices are no longer human.

Now, with the advent of nuclear and thermonuclear means, the only legitimate expression of a necessary form of a general form of warfare has been resistance up to or beyond nuclear defense against a foe whose threat is an expression of a modern technological form of oligarchical interest. All other forms of warfare or its like, are actionably criminal, clearly so if the violator is of the quality of the current British imperially reigning oligarchy and its allied puppets. That evil oligarchical expression must be defeated, and, thereupon, excised from positions of power, at all necessary risk.

Otherwise, there were no just reason to license warfare. The British empire is the most likely true cause for waging such forms of warfare of resistance beyond those of necessary restoration of peace, and, hopefully, durably peaceful accommodation among sovereign nation-state republics.

Nonetheless, despite the aforesaid restrictions against warfare or mass-murderous actions such as those just conducted in Libya, especially the war-criminal quality of the crimes condoned by President Barack Obama and others in those unconstitutional and related forms of unlawful forms of action taken by Obama in the instance of Libya, it was, in this case, the Obama administration and its relevant accomplices which were, de facto, and also U.S. Constitutionally, the party of evil.

The Criminality of Obama

Two crucial sets of facts must be added to those aforesaid issues of the case at hand. First, the conduct of

President Obama is a remarkably exact image of the character and expressed practices of the Roman Emperor Nero, as defined by LaRouche, in his April 11, 2009 webcast.

President Obama as the leading feature of the policies launched under his reign which are Adolf-Hitler-like crimes against humanity taken by Obama under British royal influence. Second, and no less significant, it has been fully demonstrated in fact, as by me personally since April 2009, that President Obama is, in a fully functional sense, not only a remarkably exact image of the character and expressed practices of the Roman Emperor Nero, but that my explicit exposure of those Nero-like actions of Obama which were precisely defined by me, had been already stated with relatively full and great precision, in the course of my report to that international webcast. There is nothing in Obama's character, as of the present day, which I had not identified with precision during that April 2009 web-cast.

I have made numerous fully validated major economic and related forecasts, in my role as an economist since my Summer 1956 forecast of a late-February-early-March 1957, very deep U.S. recession to erupt at that forecast time. My persistent warning since 1966 of a likely major U.S. monetary crisis which had occurred in August 1971, was, notably, contrary to all notable other relatively notable economists, and to numerous others, at later times up to the present moment. I would rank the great precision of my April 2009 forecast of the character of President Obama, as having been the most precise, and most significant of virtually all the forecasts which I had made up to approximately the present date.

If Barack Obama is not impeached out of office very soon, not only will there not be a still-existing United States very, very soon, but the kind of mass-murder which struck ancient Rome under the later days of the Emperor Nero; there will be a scale of mass-murder comparable to, but far more extensive than that which the citizens of ancient Rome experienced from the Emperor Nero. The details of the likeness of Obama to the Emperor Nero is one of the greatest of likenesses to the Emperor Nero in all well-known history of trans-Atlantic civilization.

The exactitude of the likeness of Obama to the mass-murderous Emperor Nero, is so exact in details, that it is already certain that the British monarchy, which actually placed Obama in the Presidency, must have found in Obama its choice of a prospective U.S. occupant of the Presidency who must have been most carefully pre-selected as the type of psychotic personally selected to bring about the self-destruction of the United States.

Therefore, I have privately made an additional forecast of future history, which I shall withhold from public circulation at this time.

That much said in this chapter this far, I shall now proceed with the essential foresight into the presently accelerating economic crisis as such.

The Physical Science of Forecasting

The most typically incompetent form of economic forecasting, is premised on the presumption that the introduction of a new physical principle, is necessarily to be located within the specific time and place within which that forecast is first made. That blundering presumption has depended largely on the current prevalent, incompetent presumption of such sources as what are to be regarded as such "authorities" as the notorious Adam Smith found among modern British economists, their dupes and other followers.

The fact is, that any true discovery of principle is expressed only along the course of the lapse of time which has led to both the introduction and implementation of that discovery. In practical terms, that historical fact is presently the most important discovery in physical science up through any present that the lapsed time leading into the discovery and its realization, has been in the process during which its initialization and fulfillment have occurred. The presumption that physical time is a matter of specific "clock time," has been one of the most perniciously significant, but, nonetheless, one of the most popular and important delusions in the popular practice of physical science still today.

Thus, as I had emphasized in the course of the questions and answers of my recent September 30 th national address, that any actually true discovery of a principle changes the lawful characteristics of any specific character of contemporary physical time.

This quality of change is known to us, presently, only as a characteristic of specifically human behavior within the bounds of a physical space-time, rather than that defined as "clock time." For this purpose, we must place the emphasis on effects which correspond to a discovery of universal physical principles as such, or those comparable principles which are to be classified as either human-generated actions on the universe, or on the specific consequences of the experiencing of those specific qualities of actions.

The latter qualifications demand a bit of emphasis on explanations.

For example:

No physical principle could exist as if in something tantamount to the hypothetical notion of a physical principle of action existing within "empty space." There are no "stand-alone principles" existing which actually correspond to "a principle in any quality of space other than its own," nor is there any existence of "empty space." There is only action in "physical time," and as expressed in terms of reference to "physical time."

In effect, the characteristic of the human species is the willful change as actions which change the system of "physical time."[11]

All of those preceding matters of emphasis are absolutely indispensable for any comprehensive apprehen-

sion of the ordering of human activity within the universe. Without that specific quality of development in physical science and its correlatives, there is no competent scientific practice in general. On this account, the conception of relativity, as of Albert Einstein and those of comparable, anti-Bertrand Russell practices, is indispensable, scientifically, for all subject-matters. The notion of physically relative time is indispensable for a competently, generally progressive notion of the physical universe in physical, rather than simply clock-time.

The Practical Implications

During a lapsed time which has occupied much of the recent dozen months of our "Basement" activity, since our August 2010 abandonment of the existence of a primitive's notion of the existence of what had been damned by relevant actually leading scientists since more than a century ago, we had good reason to join in damning the silly notion of "space by itself" and "time by itself." Our same "Basement" crew responsible for most of this scientific research, has expended considerable, relatively comprehensive attention on approximately a half-billion years scrutiny of the leading re-

Lyndon LaRouche's university textbook on national economic policy, which also serves as a manual for government officials and advisors to governments.

---

11. As in entering the revolutionary (physical-economic mode) specific to the culture of a new century. It is the act of the qualitative change in mode which inhabits the specific quality of action befitting a notion of " 'physical time,' as qualitatively distinct from 'clock time'."

LPAC

"The principal obstacle to comprehension of the issues of a science of physical economy today, has been, scientifically, relatively impotent doctrines of 'clock-time.'" Now, the LaRouche "Basement Team," is continuing LaRouche's earlier discoveries in that sphere, as well as developing collaborative relationships with international scientific circles. Shown: Jason Ross presents a class on Riemann and Abelian functions, in an LPAC video (http://larouchepac.com/riemann2b).

cords of the subject of the series of evolutionary development of living species, their origins, their existence, and the related evolutionary history. Most of the evidence treated in this process, is to be fairly considered as factually standard as presently known as fairly modern "catholic" evidence, as familiar to, relatively speaking, the most highly qualified sources employed on behalf of our team's own original work in this and closely related fields.

The most profound among the implications of this line of investigations, has corresponded to the fruits of my own, original earlier advances in the notion of the principles of physical space-time as such, especially as situated within the domain of the science of the specific considerations of physical economy. The principal obstacle to comprehension of the issues of a science of physical economy today, has been, scientifically, relatively impotent doctrines of "clock-time." Whereas the notion of physical time itself, has been a relatively long-standing conception of my own independent work, the situation of my own, earlier discoveries and practice within the context of our "Basement" crew, has been a crucially important setting for both the continuing of my own earlier discoveries on this account, and the great benefit of collaboration with my "Basement" associates, especially since the Summer of 2010. The "Basement" has represented the true principle of a virtually daily functioning team, rather than a mere collection of separate bodies expressing related interests. More and more, that team's activities have been extended, quite naturally, toward international scientific circles of collaborative, specific scientific interests shared in common.

Admittedly, teams of similar qualities have become long since traditional among the best qualities of academic and related scientific circles and teams back to the times of such original modern scientists as Filippo Brunelleschi, Cardinal Nicholas of Cusa, and the pack of modern geniuses among such explicit followers of Cusa, and his greatest followers in the domain of physical science, such as the greatest of them as Leonardo da Vinci and Johannes Kepler. However, the explicit function of physical space-time, as I have identified that here, has lacked any adequate semblance of treatment of the actual notion of physical time, as distinct from a rare kind of clock-time up to the present time.

Such was the concept which I had presented in the answers to the questions presented to me in the course of the recent September 30th national broadcast. and in the already designated LPAC *Weekly Report* of Wednesday, October 19 th .

Much more on those same stated lines of inquiry is to be said and written in the course of the remaining time yet to come.

China Plans $4.7 Billion Renovation of Haitian Capital

by Cynthia R. Rush

Sept. 5 (EIRNS)—On Aug. 25, Ralph Youri Chevy, mayor of the Haitian capital, Port-au-Prince, formally accepted a $4.7 billion proposal from China's Southwest Municipal Engineering Design and Research Institute (SMEDRIC), to renovate and rebuild that city, including its port, over the next three years, providing all the infrastructure required to modernize the capital and uplift its impoverished population. This nation of ten million, which shares the island of Hispaniola with the Dominican Republic, has never recovered from the effects of the January 2010 earthquake that killed 250,000 people, injured tens of thousands more, and wiped out what little infrastructure existed.

Although financing for the renovation is not yet pinned down, journalist Georgeanne Nienaber noted in an Aug. 27 article in *The Huffington Post* that "China has made good on similar projects in its estimated trillion-dollar Silk Road initiative, not to mention 30 futuristic infrastructure projects in its own country. Perhaps the future has finally arrived for Haiti, and as a result, the Caribbean corridor will be transformed." Telesur news agency reported Sept. 1 that the initial idea for the project was conceived of at the May 14-15 summit of the Belt and Road Initiative in Beijing.

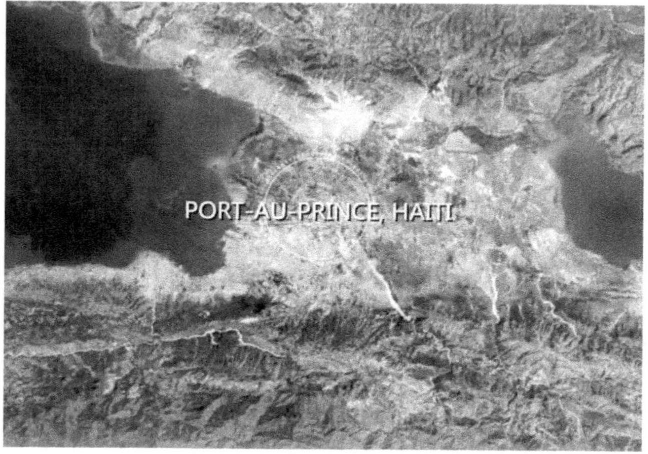

All graphics are from SMEDRIC's video illustrating the Port-au-Prince project.

Illustration of areas most in need of reconstruction and modernization, some never rebuilt since the 2010 earthquake.

Obama the Killer

The Chinese proposal stands in stark contrast to the criminal actions of the Obama Administration and allied "Western donors," who rejected the proposals made by American statesman Lyndon LaRouche in February 2010, by which the U.S. would sign a 25-year bilateral treaty with the Haitian government to rebuild the nation, based on an emergency deployment of the Army Corps of Engineers (USACE) and other military and civilian agencies with expertise in responding to natural disasters. The immediate priority at that time was to relocate to higher ground, the almost two million homeless earthquake victims stranded in Port-au-Prince, with the necessary medical and other services, before the arrival of the rainy season brought another wave of mass deaths.

During a Jan. 30, 2010 international webcast, LaRouche warned that "you cannot apply a band-aid to Haiti, because the objective is, if the country is going to be viable … you have to have a sovereign Haiti." Haitians, he added, have been "subjected to all kinds of terrible history; … promised this, and betrayed, and promised that, and betrayed, and promised and betrayed…. So, it's a model approach: we make a contract with the government, as a treaty agreement between the

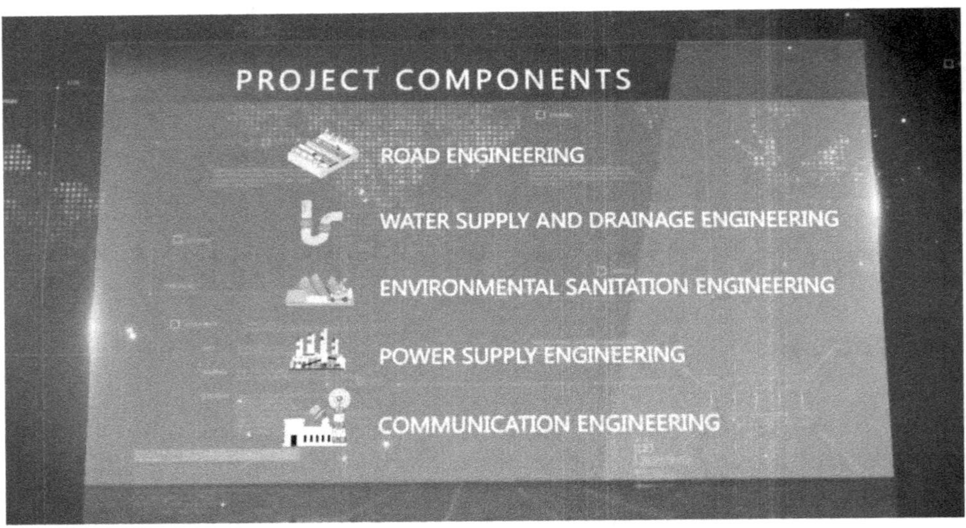

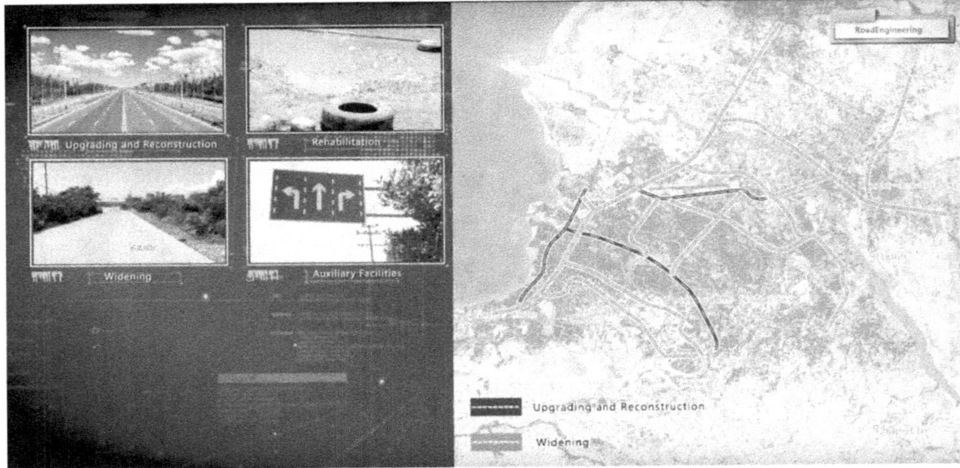

Upgrading, reconstruction and widening of transportation facilities.

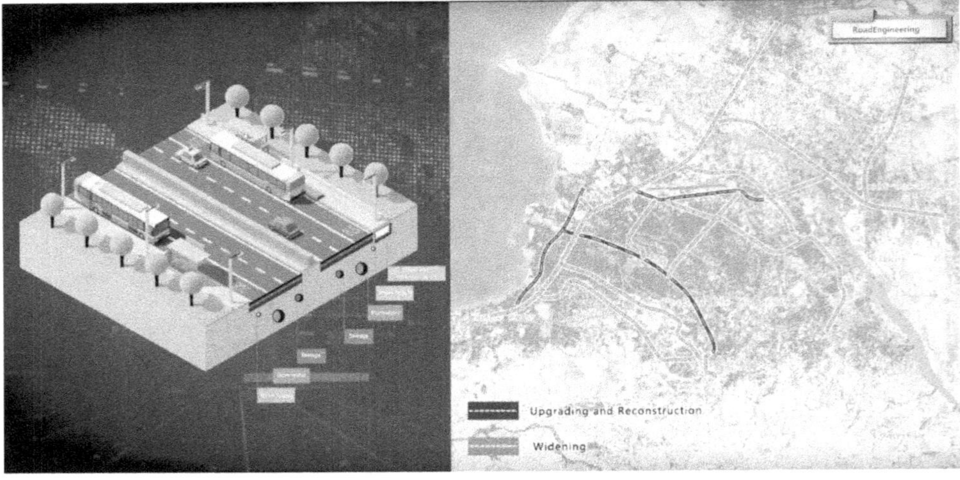

Road drainage with water supply, stormwater, sewage, and power and communication conduits.

United States and Haiti, to assure the rebuilding of their country, in a form in which it will actually be a functioning country which can survive."

Barack Obama took the path of betrayal. Reliable sources told *EIR* in late February 2010 that a group of American "old hands" on Haiti agreed with LaRouche's proposals and presented them to Obama, who rejected them out of hand. After allowing a very short term deployment of the USACE and medical facilities such as the U.S.S. Comfort, he handed the relief effort over to an army of competing non-governmental organizations (NGOs), whose activities and corruption ensured there would be no recovery in Haiti. For years afterward, homeless citizens remained "housed" in precarious tents in the center of the capital, or sent back to live in unsafe structures damaged by the earthquake.

Given conditions on the ground, the cholera outbreak that occurred in October of that year was entirely predictable. To date, this waterborne disease has infected 800,000 Haitians, killing close to 10,000. The necessary sanitation infrastructure—sewage treatment and guarantee of safe drinking water—was never built, and every new hurricane or tropical storm hitting the island brings disease and destruc-

Flood protection for water levels occurring rarely in a century.

Flood interception trenches handle water levels happening rarely in 50 years.

Rainwater collecting system designed to drain largest storms of a three-year time interval.

tion in its wake.

As National Public Radio reported July 17, Port-au-Prince is one of the largest cities in the world without a central sewage system. The majority of the capital's three million residents use out-houses, and much of the waste ends up in canals, ditches, and other unsanitary dumping grounds where it can contaminate drinking water and spread disease. There is only one open-air sewage treatment plant in the *entire country*, located in Morne Cabrit, about an hour from downtown Port-au-Prince.

A New Capital

The renovation proposed by China's Southwestern Municipal Engineering and Design Institute, which is part of a $30 billion package offered by China to develop all of Haiti, will address these problems. It is divided into six sub-projects, involving water and drainage works, road improvements, environmental protections, drainage and sanitation, a communications network, transportation, and recon-struction of the historic "old city" of Port-au-Prince.

According to Georgeanne Nienaber, drainage engineer-ing will be primary, with flood interception trenches and rainwater runoff collec-tion systems routed to rivers and the ocean. A water puri-fication plant capable of han-dling 225,000 cubic meters

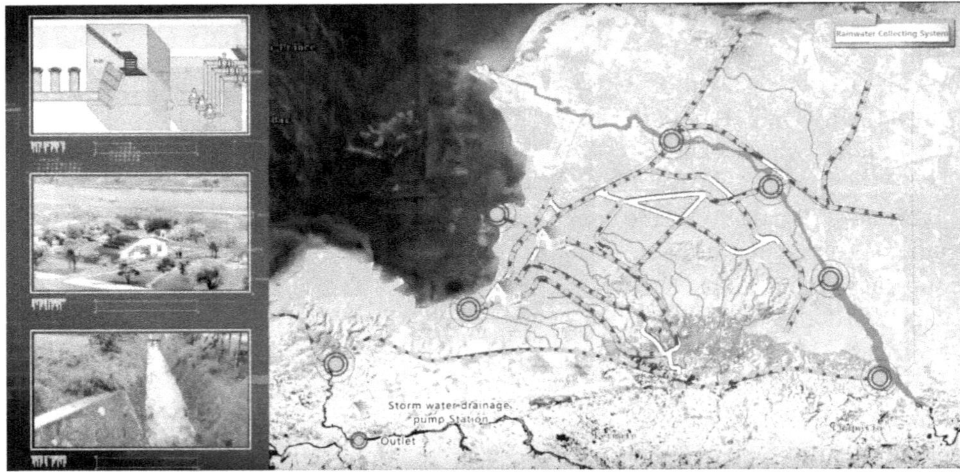

The rainwater is collected by pipeline and discharged along the rivers.

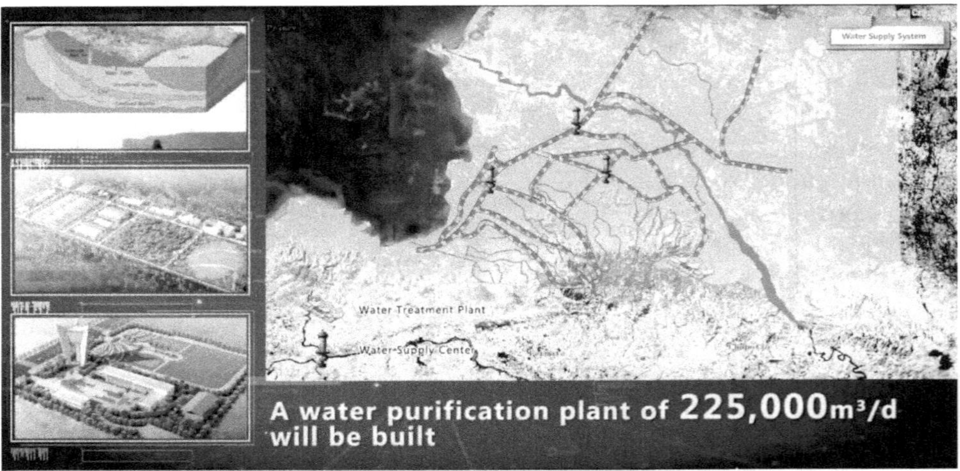

A water purification plant of 225,000 cubic meters per day will be built in the urban area.

Environmental sanitation in public areas such as stations, parks and residential areas.

per day will be built, to ensure a supply of safe drinking water. A new sewage plant will treat 18,000 cubic meters per day to "required standards and be discharged along the rivers and sea," according to project engineers. A new gas-fired power station has a planned 2,000 MW output.

The renovation plan includes installing 450 public toilets, and implementing a public garbage collection system and waste landfills, which will accept 1,500 tons per day for domestic waste.

Nienaber reports that work is expected to begin in December on a variety of sanitation, power, communications, and other projects in the capital, for which 20,000 workers will have to be hired. A beautiful, optimistic video of the renovation project was released by the Haitian firm Bati Aiyti, which will be partnering with Chinese firms to complete the project, to create "a brilliant future" for the city, as the video states.

Many other Caribbean nations are also looking forward to "a brilliant future" with China's help. Jamaica, Trinidad & Tobago, Barbados, Guyana, and Cuba are among the governments that have signed major agreements with the Chinese government, or Chinese state-sector companies or private entities, to build needed infrastructure.

Power supply engineering, and upgrading of the distribution networks.

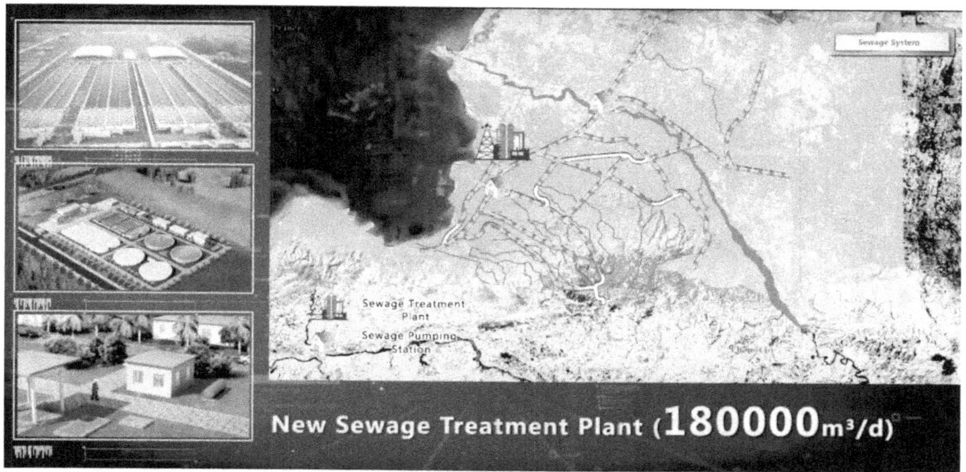

Sewage treatment plant and sewage pumping station.

Construction of new housing is urgently needed.

Syrian Reconstruction Ready for Takeoff

by Ulf Sandmark, *EIR* Stockholm correspondent

Central Damascus is a beautiful and busy city.

The support for the International Trade Fair from the Syrian people was massive, with 300,000 visitors a day.

Sept. 4—The incredible momentum of the Syrian Armed Forces in reconquering vast regions of Syrian territory from ISIS and other terrorist groups, is energizing the Syrian economic recovery. With only four months' lead time, the Syrian government organized the reopening of the Damascus International Trade Fair to kick off the restarting of the economy. *EIR* took part in this historic event through its Stockholm correspondent, Ulf Sandmark, who visited the fair as part of a 25-person delegation of Swedish businessmen.

This was the 59th Damascus International Trade Fair since its inception in 1954, after a five year-hiatus during the war. It turned out to be a huge success, with exhibitors from 45 nations and overwhelming popular support, flooding the fair grounds with 300,000 visitors a day. The Syrian people were eager to see the full scope of Syria's productive powers—the famous Syrian food and textile industries, as well as the chemical and engineering industries. There were also two pavillions relaunching the Syrian heritage of artisans and handicraft. On display were the industries that had been kept going throughout the war, in many cases on a 24-hour basis, joined by restarted industries like the Khallouf Trading Company, which in February 2017 resumed its Hama car manufacturing plant in partnership with the Chinese Dongfeng Motor Company.

EIR met with the highest Syrian government representatives, bringing them the full scope of Lyndon La-

Rouche's Four Laws policy (here in Arabic) in the form of the Arabic translation by Hussein Askary, of *EIR*'s World Landbridge Special Report. *EIR* took part in a meeting at the Prime Minister's office, where representatives of many of the nations of the old Silk Road renewed their commitment to cooperation with Syria —a truly historical moment. Syrian Prime Minister Imad Khamis, with a big smile, received his own copy of the *EIR* Special Report. Sandmark subsequently met with the Minister of Tourism Eng. Besher Yazji, with the Director General of the Syrian Investment Agency, Dr. Inas al-Omawi, and other high officials. A special donation, by a very prominent Swedish *EIR* subscriber, of 15 copies of the World Land-Bridge Special Report in Arabic for the universities in Damascus and Aleppo, was delivered to the President of Damascus University, Prof. Dr. M. Hassan al-Kurdi. In total, 40 copies were brought to Syria.

The Special Report, with its added chapter, "Phoenix Project Syria: Discussion Points on the Reconstruction of Syria," will provide crucial input for Syrian economic policy making. See the video about the Phoenix project in the context of the reconstruction of Aleppo. It has also been covered on this Syrian site.

The challenges for Syria are enormous after the devastation of more than six years of war. The World bank has estimated that the war destruction in Syria amounts to U.S. $320 billion. The rebuilding of Syria will definitely require a credit system, taking into consideration that millions of Syrians, especially in youth brigades, need to be put to work in the coming year to maintain the momentum needed to unify the nation and keep peace. A government effort in a New Deal style will be crucial.

The Friends of Syria has already begun projects to restart the economy. Russia, beside all diplomatic, military and civilian aid, has restarted the coastal railway line and is aiding in the restarting of the petroleum in-

Syrian Prime Minister Imad Khamis receives the EIR special report in Arabic, The New Silk Road Becomes the World Landbridge.

The Political and Media Advisor of the President of Syria, Bouthaina Shaaban (center), with the Schiller Institute's Talal Moualla (left) and the author.

Dr. Inas al-Omawi (left), Director General of the Syrian Investment Agency (SIA) for foreign investors, with the author (right), Syrian representative of the Schiller Institute Mr. Talal Moualla, and delegation member Aly El Khosht. SIA is part of the Office of the Prime Minister and is located in the beautiful, old-style building where the prime minister formerly resided.

Syria Tourism Minister Eng. Besher Yazji (second from left) received the author (right), Syrian representative of the Schiller Institute Mr. Talal Moualla, and delegation member Aly El Khosht (far left).

dustry. Iran is committed to bring industries, like the one they restarted in 2015 for the production of the Syrian car Sham. China will help rebuild all airports, then the railway system, and subsequently the highway system.

However, the main effort rests on the shoulders of the Syrian nation, which under the leadership of President Dr. Bashar Assad, has conducted the war in the spirit of nationbuilding. The sovereignty of Syria has been asserted with continuous efforts to keep strong national institutions functioning for public services in all sectors. Reconstruction has been ongoing in huge public work projects, during the war. Territories under government control during the war have been repaired and are fully functioning, including the construction of entirely new Damascus suburbs.

The reconstruction of the devastated areas, that used to be occupied by the terrorists, is now fully underway. Every damaged house we saw when travelling in the Damascus suburbs, was under repair, with new walls going up. This is the secret behind the success of the Syrian Arab Army. It is not only because of the support of the military allies, but because of a nationbuilding effort *working* for victory, with the Syrian population working non-stop to keep their nation functioning: the baker making bread, and health workers, teachers, and school kids doing their part to keep the nation going. The salary for such a public servant is now about U.S. $50-60 per *month*.

No greater testimony to the broad popular support of the President can be given than this continuing mobilization of an absolute majority of the Syrian people, including the millions of internal refugees who fled into government-controlled areas. It can also be seen in the accelerating national reconciliation process, which is bringing back thousands of former armed rebels to resettle and resume their citizen status, taking up their work in society and sometimes also in the army, to fight their former military allies. At least 600,000 refugees, mainly from Aleppo, have returned to their homes to rebuild.

A Deadly Attack Against the International Trade Fair

This war mobilization—of the people, by the people and for the people—is the only way to explain the absolutely remarkable reaction by visitors to the Trade Fair

Every destroyed apartment house that could be seen in the Damascus war zones, formerly occupied by gunmen, was under repair.

The high-quality Syrian handicraft sector is relaunched as a policy. Here an artisan shows handmade rugs from Aleppo.

Scania Trucks and Buses was represented at the Damascus International Trade Fair through Iran. Here, the author (left) with Nidal Hana, head of the Hanagroup, which owns the Scania manufacturer in Iran.

to the deadly attack against its entrance. This attack is significant, and it was the only news in most of the Western world media about the remarkable Damascus International Trade Fair.

The terrorists from a nearby terrorist-controlled suburb, on the fourth day of the Trade Fair, launched a grenade from a grenade launcher, hitting the side of the entrance building of the Fair Grounds. Nine people died and many were wounded when the the grenade hit the stone pavement and spread deadly shrapnel. Among the the dead were a female export manager and her husband. Later this author inspected the traces of shrapnel on the building and the broken windows.

However, when the Swedish delegation arrived a few hours after the attack, the entrance was crowded with people. The Trade Fair was

The BRICS nations and Asia were massively present. The South Korean Kioti tractors at the Damascus Trade Fair are shown here.

not shutdown or evacuated. This is the fighting spirit of the population, who continued to come to the Fair Grounds by the hundreds of thousands every day. People wanted to celebrate and take part in the economic recovery of their nation, and would not allow terrorists stop them. They trusted the army to hit back and no further attack was launched against the fair. The whole fair grounds was furthermore under an anti-missile protection shield covering the nearby airport.

The terrorists had broken a deconfliction agreement with the Russians. It is the so-called "moderate" terrorists who have made such agreements, not the other Al-Qaeda-linked group in the occupied Eastern Ghouta

Damascus suburb. These "moderates" are the terrorists providing the territorial basis for Mohammad Alloush, of the Jaish al-Islam faction, who is a member of the High Negotiations Committee (HNC), which is leading the opposition delegation in the UN-led peace negotiations in Geneva, as well as in the negotiations in Astana. He has been supported by the Western world, including Sweden, in his role as negotiator for the Syrian "opposition."

Throughout the war, most of Damascus has been a war zone, where terrorists, from time to time, randomly send grenades from their area, Jobar, just outside the Old City, and from Eastern Ghouta a little further away.

The Damascus 59th International Trade Fair became a people's festival celebrating the Syrian revival.

The population takes its losses and fights back, working and supporting the army to protect them. The repair work is being done much faster than in Europe. In a visit by this author in 2015, passing by a street crossing attacked the day before, all traces were cleaned up. The wrecked cars had been towed off. Only some new asphalt, and damage to trees nearby, revealed the attack the day before.

This time, on Sunday, Aug. 30, this author heard two grenades hit central Damascus at two different occasions and places. When hearing these grenade explosions, the Syrian people in the streets just shook their heads silently and kept on with their business. Three nights in a row at midnight, the Syrian army, for twenty minutes, fired a special new type of missile that can reach the terrorist tunnels in Eastern Ghouta; even then, the people in the street did not blink an eye.

The Use of Terrorism for 'Diplomacy'

The terrorists cling to these remaining territories in the Damascus area, hiding in huge tunnel systems for months. They have no military significance at all beyond the capacity to launch terrorist attacks. The occupation of this slice of territory in the Syrian capital is pure cabinet warfare, used for diplomatic purposes, to try to continue the UN negotiations in Geneva, which were intended to bring down Syrian President Dr. Bashar al-Assad and bring chaos as in Libya. These terrorists have helped Western intelligence services stage incidents for international consumption, trying to bring the United States into an open war against the Syrian (and Russian) governments. The most famous was the gas attack in Eastern Ghouta in 2013, where the videos from the incident displayed dead bodies of children, but these were children kidnapped much earlier from an entirely different part of Syria.

The terrorists have brought nothing but destruction, and they oppress the local population in terrorist-held areas, putting women and children in metal cages, on the roofs of buildings as human shields, to prevent their bases and offices from being attacked. They know the Syrian government would not attack women. These hold-outs will soon come to an end. The Syrian Arab Army has been making steady progress in reconquering these suburbs, which are the last Damascus area suburbs remaining in terrorist hands after the recent victory by the combined forces of the Lebanese Army, Hezbollah, and the Syrian Arab Army on the Lebanese border in Qalamoun district. All other areas have been cleared by military campaigns in combination with reconciliation negotiations, where terrorists agreed either to be bussed away to friends in other Syrian areas, or to give up their weapons and settle accounts, and the question of their citizenship, with the Syrian state.

The military campaigns and the genial reconciliation process is about to outflank the UN-led Geneva peace talks. This entirely domestic peace process soon will have settled the conflict, so there will be no more reconciliation to talk about in Geneva. However, after a final military victory, the most difficult part of the domestic peace process will have to proceed for a long time. As Minister of Reconciliation Ali Heidary said: "It is only when the mother of the martyr is reconciled

The more than one-hundred-year-old Damascus university is one of the typical, strong backbone institutions of Syria, with 200,000 day students and 70,000 in the evening. It has been open throughout the war in spite of grenade attacks. In the campus park, a monument commemorates the martyred teachers and students.

plish with the help of their banks. They will try to rob the Syrian people of their economic sovereignty, create a new economic crisis, fuel dissent and restart the troubles. With their control of international banks and the financial system, they will try to continue the economic embargo aiming to freeze the nation economically, as they did with the victorious nation of Bosnia Herzegovina in former Yugoslavia which, within the Dayton agreement, was not allowed to control its own Central Bank. That action had blocked its economic development until the recent Chinese action to start huge development programs there.

The difference is just that. Unlike Bosnia and Herzegovina, Syria has been asserting its sovereignty and has friends, like the BRICS countries, as well as among its regional neighbors. However, all financing for reconstruction cannot come from abroad or from rich Syrians in exile. The government absolutely needs a credit system to control the credit flows of the banks to be able to put Syrian industrialists, businessmen, farmers, artisans, and new entrepreneurs, deprived of all resources in the war, back in business. The same goes for putting millions of returning refugees to work, to be able to make a living and rebuild their lives. Likewise for putting young people into work training programs in youth brigades, to integrate the nation in a huge reconstruction effort, as Franklin D. Roosevelt did with the New Deal and the Civil Conservation Corps for youth.

The crucial input of the Four Laws of Lyndon LaRouche in the context of the New Silk Road/World Land-Bridge will therefore be decisive in keeping up the momentum of victory and the full realization of Syrian sovereignty. Syria is now in a full "war mobilization" with its nation-building measures. This puts Syria in the best position to launch a credit system and a New Deal policy to take care of all of its desperately poor—but hopeful—people, people now coming out of the newly liberated but devastated war regions formerly occupied by terrorists.

with the mother of the murderer, that the country will come to peace."

The Need for a Credit System

The government will have something like a year after the war to bring the people together and take care of its most vulnerable citizens. In that one-year period, millions of Syrians will have to be put to work. Economic development will have to reach all areas, especially areas where there has been dissent. Otherwise Syria will explode again.

Even though the guns of the rebels will have been turned in to the government, the nation will still be full of hidden arms and experienced fighters. Before the war, the economic conditionalities of the International Monetary Fund created austerity for the Syrian population and an economic crisis, which fueled the protests in the heavily orchestrated Arab Spring in Syria.

The British imperial powers and their international coalition will not take a military victory by the Syrian nation and its heroic President easily. *EIR* emphasized in all discussions with Syrian officials that what the British empire could not achieve by military means, with the help of their terrorists, they will try to accom-

The Manifest Destiny of China and America

by Robert Wesser

This article was originally published in The New Federalist, *on March 27, 2000. Since that date, we have witnessed 9/11 and its aftermath, wars in Iraq, Afghanistan, Syria and elsewhere, the catastrophic Bush and Obama Presidencies, the great depression beginning in 2007-08, and the unprecedented emergence of China as a force for global economic development through its Belt and Road Initiative. Today's world is a much different place from that of seventeen years ago. Nevertheless, despite certain references to the political environment which existed at the time of its original appearance, EIR's decision to republish this article is motivated by the critical importance of the American-Chinese relationship at this moment in history. Mr. Wesser's research into the history and nature of both America and China in the period from the Washington through Grant Presidencies is an invaluable contribution toward demonstrating the common aims of both nations, both in a previous era as well as for the future before us. Below is a slightly edited version of the original.*

*   *   *   *

As has been widely covered in this newspaper, the Y2000 Presidential campaign of Democratic Party pre-candidate Lyndon LaRouche has unleashed a growing movement in the United States to steer this nation away from its present, disastrous course, back to its true Manifest Destiny—to be the Beacon of Hope, and Temple of Liberty for all mankind. This mission is nothing less than a 2,500 year battle to secure a form of government, the Nation State, whereby all people must enjoy the most fundamental of inalienable rights. In LaRouche's words:

The right of every human being is to live in such way, that they, in their own way, can have their powers of reason cultivated, can find something good to do for humanity, so that they can die with a smile on their face, because they die with the assurance that in the life they had, they have secured a permanent place, and identity for themselves, in the simultaneity of eternity.

LaRouche's call for a New Bretton Woods monetary system, based on a Community of Nations in common agreement with this fundamental understanding of the true nature of man, requires a strategic partnership with those nations which currently represent the vast majority of the human population on this planet. Those nations, led by the "strategic triangle" of Russia, India, and China, must now ally with the United States and Western Europe to implement a durable, worldwide economic recovery. Presidential candidate LaRouche's New Bretton Woods/Eurasian landbridge policy is,

Lincoln and Sun Yat-sen on a U.S. postage stamp during World War II.

therefore, nothing less than a global war-winning strategy for securing such a true, human identity for all of mankind.

As LaRouche has described in detail, this mission, America's true Manifest Destiny—originating with Classical Greece culture, and advanced through the Christian apostolic mission and 15th century Golden Renaissance—has consistently driven American patriots *westward*, from New England across the American continent and into the Pacific and Asia.

To this end, the following report is the first in a series aimed at introducing the reader to some of the "forgotten men and women" of this history: the American patriots and their Chinese counterparts who sought to create a modern China by initiating a great dialogue between the ancient wisdom of Confucius, and the revolutionary ideas of the United States Constitution.

Historically, this fruitful partnership emerged through a very simple "common interest": the resounding defeat of the British Empire, and of oligarchism as a whole.

American Missionaries Go to China

...take some notice of the changes taking place ... in Asiatic Russia, in the countries bordering upon China on the west and south, in other countries besides our own in the New World, and in the numerous fertile islands of the Pacific Ocean, both in the smaller central groups and in those which separate it from the Indian Ocean, and which approach continents in magnitude, and in variety and extent of the products of their soils and mines. *The destiny of these parts of the world and of the races which inhabit them, is to be decided by the influences that shall proceed from the United States and China.*

—American missionary
Rev. William Speer, 1870

In 1810, a group of patriotic Americans led by Rev. Jedediah Morse established the American Board of Commissioners of Foreign Missionaries (ABCFM) at Farmington, Connecticut. Much of the initial missionary leadership of the ABCFM had been the veterans of fierce battles between Americans and the British over the control of the New York State frontier. The British (as well as the French) were notorious for organizing brutalized Indian factions to conduct terrorist-style massacres of pro-independence frontier settlements, all to further their "colonial" interests. To counter the pernicious effects of this deliberate British corruption and exploitation of native American Indians, these early American missionaries established schools and other educational projects, especially in the field of agricultural improvements. To Morse and his American missionaries, native Americans were not "savages" to be culled and herded like cattle:

> The mental quality of the [native] American are not in the least inferior to those of the Europeans; that they are capable of all, even the most abstract sciences; and if equal care was taken of their education... we would see rise among the [native] Americans, philosophers, mathematicians, and divines who would rival the first of Europe.

In the tradition of early revolutionary republican Puritan leaders like John Winthrop and Cotton Mather, Morse and his ABCFM missionaries understood Christianity not as a "personal religious question" or "feeling," but rather as a profound philosophical passion to "do good works" through spreading the cause of the American Revolution. After the British takeover and subversion of Harvard College, Morse had set up a separate Theological Seminary at Andover in 1805. The Andover Seminary served as the recruitment and educational base of operations for a new American project: the ABCFM. By centralizing various denominations of American Revolution-oriented Christian missionaries into a single virtual army, the ABCFM would now deploy *internationally* to evangelize the world on behalf of what China missionary William Speer would later describe as the "School of Nations," the United States of the Declaration of Independence and the Constitution of 1789.

Morse's conception of the ABCFM spread rapidly throughout other patriotic American networks, especially those associated with Benjamin Franklin's Philadelphia-based American Philosophical Society. A good example was that of ABCFM founding board member Elias Boudinot IV. In the 1750s, Boudinot's father had collaborated with Benjamin Franklin to build Philadelphia's Second Presbyterian Church. In 1772, a young man from the Island of St. Croix named Alexander Hamilton was recruited to come to America by Franklin Society "graduate" Rev. Hugh Knox. The

John Quincy Adams
1767-1848

John Jay
1745-1829

painting by Thomas Sully, 1816
Elias Boudinot

Library of Congress
Theodore Frelinghuysen

Frelinghuysen entered the U.S. Senate from New Jersey. Frelinghuysen went on to become the leading national advocate of the American Christian missionary movement, later serving as ABCFM president from 1847-59.

In 1829, the year that Theodore Frelinghuysen entered the Senate, the ABCFM had deployed 25 year-old New Brunswick, New Jersey native David Abeel to southern China, assigned "to begin his work with western sailors" as ABCFM Chaplain of the American Seamen's Friend Society. Abeel had graduated from the Theological Seminary of the American Dutch Reformed Church in New Brunswick, where he was recruited to the ABCFM "army" for foreign mission work. Thirteen years later, the very same ABCFM "Friend Society" position would land Rev. Samuel Chenery Damon in Hawaii, where his son Frank went on to become a personal collaborator of Sun Yat-sen's Hawaiian-based 1911 Republican Revolution.

In addition to Abeel, other 19th Century American missionary operatives sent to China included:

• American Presbyterian Board member James C. Hepburn, associated with the Amoy hospital at the same time Abeel was in China in the 1840's. A graduate of the University of Pennsylvania, Hepburn became famous for standardizing a romanized system for the Japanese language. He was later sent to Japan in 1859 as part of the U.S.-Japan Harris Treaty operations, responsible for organizing the well-known Meiji Restoration and subsequent American system-sponsored industrialization of Japan. Hepburn is still known in Japan today as the founder of the Meiji Gakuin University.

• Rev. S.R. Brown, of Springfield, Massachusetts, responsible for organizing the first delegation of Chinese students brought to the United States in 1847 for a complete Western education. One of Brown's students, Yung Wing from Macao, became the first Chinese to

young Hamilton was sent to live with the Boudinot family in New Jersey, where he was further groomed for a leading role in the cause of the American revolution. Future ABCFM board member Elias Boudinot IV, became a leading member of George Washington's inner circle and, as a congressman from New Jersey, was responsible for proposing and securing the appointment of Hamilton as first Secretary of the Treasury in 1789.

Another national figure in the ABCFM was New Jersey's Theodore Frelinghuysen. Theodore's father, Frederick F. Frelinghuysen, had commanded artillery in the Revolutionary War, and had led the battle for New Jersey's ratification of the U.S. Constitution, serving as U.S. Senator from 1793-96. In 1829, Theodore graduate from an American University. Brown also went on to Japan to serve with Hepburn and others in the Meiji industrialization project.

• Philadelphia-based missionary and later Burlingame Treaty organizer William Speer, sent to China by the Presbyterian Board of Foreign Missions, where he spent six years in Canton (1852-58). Speer ended up settling in California, where he fought vigorously to enfranchise Chinese immigrant labor as full citizens, especially after the Civil War.

David Abeel, Xu Jiyu and *A Brief Analysis of the World*

To this day, visitors to the Washington Monument will find inside an extraordinary inscription portraying the first President of the United States of America:

> Of all the famous Westerners of ancient and modern times, can Washington be placed in any position but first?

The inscription is written *in Chinese*, taken from Confucian nationalist Xu Jiyu's groundbreaking 1848 work *A Brief Analysis of the World*. Despite its title, Xu's work was the most complete Chinese-authored world geographical and historical study in modern times, and was the fruit of the first major collaboration between American republicans and a high-ranking Qing Dynasty official of Confucian-nationalist persuasion.

In 1843, American missionary David Abeel first met Fujian Governor Xu Jiyu in the port city of Amoy. Later, in his memoirs, Abeel would describe Xu as:

> …the most inquisitive Chinese of a high rank I have yet met. After asking many questions about foreign countries, we proposed bringing an atlas

David Abeel

and showing him the position and extent of the places which were most interesting to him.…

He was far more anxious to learn the state of kingdoms of this world, than the truths of the kingdom of heaven.

Xu Jiyu had been born and raised in the north-central Chinese province of Shanxi, gateway to the old silk road. Descended from a long line of Confucian scholars, Xu had been steeped from early childhood in ancient Chinese history, and all of the Confucian classics. By 1843, Fujian Governor Xu Jiyu held one of the most powerful official positions in Qing Dynasty China. Fujian's principal cities were the strategic Taiwan Strait ports of Fuzhou and Xiamen (Amoy). Both cities were the historic international trading/communication centers of all southern Chinese mercantile operations throughout South Asia, and served as a home base for overseas Chinese. Fujian Province was also the historical center of Chinese resistance against the widely perceived foreign Manchu occupation of China, which was the Qing Dynasty. This resistance centered around the secret Triad Society ("overthrow the Qing, restore the Ming"), and the unusually disproportionate number of Fujian-educated Confucian scholars, whose ranks the Manchus had tapped for Qing officials.

The brutal Opium War offensive by Her Majesty's Royal Navy "to teach those Chinese a lesson about the law of free trade," had led to the imposition of the humiliating 1842 Treaty of Nanjing. As the Royal Navy bombarded China's relatively defenseless coastal cities to ruin, Hong Kong was forcibly ceded to the Empire, and the port of Shanghai forced open to foreign (i.e. British) control. The British ultimately seized four major Chinese cities (in addition to Canton), while their French *entente* allies gobbled up Vietnam, Cambodia, and Laos.

Like many of the classically-educated Confucian intelligentsia of the time, Xu's disgust at the impotence of the Manchus in the face of the Opium War onslaught against China made him hungry for new ideas. Xu's view of British, French, and Portuguese colonialism was simply that of modernized pirates "gobbling up the harbors like silkworms eating leaves."

Through 1844, American missionary David Abeel met Xu on several occasions, providing him an array of contemporary Western maps as well as thorough briefings on the world of 1844. According to Xu:

[From January to February, 1844] when I was temporarily staying in Amoy in official capacity, I met an American named Abeel. [He was] a scholar who was able to speak Fukienese and who was very well-informed regarding Western countries. He had a book of maps which were finely drawn and engraved. Unfortunately, however, I did not understand the characters. But I traced ten-odd maps and asked Abeel to transliterate them so as to get a rough idea of the pronunciation of each country.... .

Using the maps and other material provided by Abeel, Xu's *A Brief Analysis of the World* became one of the most important Chinese-language documents in the history of modern China. In the generally xenophobic world of Opium War-battered 19th Century Qing Dynasty China, Xu's analysis completely broke down all of the prevailing mythologies, superstitions, and deliberate disinformation spread about the actual state of the globe in the 1840's. Referencing Abeel's assistance and expertise many times throughout, Xu systemati-

cc/Pbwelch

Statue of Xu Jiyu in the courtyard of the Confucian Temple, Pingyao, China

cally marches the reader through nothing less than a world tour, moving from Asia, through Europe and Africa, and on to the Americas. Each section includes the most detailed possible geography, accompanied by background texts describing the history, people, culture, and religions of entire regions and countries.

The 1850 publication of *A Brief Analysis of the World* was a revolution in itself. For the first time in the modern era, the Middle Kingdom had been situated within world history and geography as a whole. Now, traditional Confucian-oriented Chinese patriots were able to access the "big picture" realities of the global conflict which characterized the post-American Revolution world—the first step toward building a modern Chinese nation-state.

'America: New Nations Against Europe'

Entitled "America: new nations against Europe," the final section of *A Brief Analysis of the World* indicates Xu Jiyu's enlightened view of China's antidote to British colonial slavery. The maps and accompanying text describe a vast American continent, originally colonized by the European powers, which now had states strong enough to *throw off* European domination. Xu describes that this new world gave birth to George Washington, founder of the United States, whose system of government the Latin American states were now following as an example. Xu notes that *only the poorer lands of America* (i.e., Canada) still remained under European control.

One can only surmise the utter horror which beset the minds of Chinese-language-literate British operatives of the Opium War era, upon reading this concluding section:

> When the people rebelled against Britain, they insisted that Washington be made commander-in-chief. This situation arose very suddenly so that weapons, gun powder, provisions, and fodder were all lacking. But Washington encouraged the people with his patriotic zeal. When the arrangements had been made, they besieged a large city. Suddenly a great wind arose, and the vessels were all scattered. Washington jumped at this chance and took the city. Later the British army assembled a great force and attacked. Washington's army was defeated and frightened; it wanted to disband and scatter. *Washington, with a sense of duty, gathered the remaining army together, and again they fought and won. The bloody war lasted for eight years with recurring setbacks, but the people were repeatedly roused to determination. Washington's resoluteness did not diminish, and the British army was becoming old.* France raised an entire army which crossed the sea. The French army and Washington's army attacked the British from both sides. Spain and Holland also checked the advance of British troops and encouraged Britain to make peace. Britain was unable to withstand, so a treaty was made with Washington. The boundary of the neighboring country [Canada] was delineated. The northern region of cold, barren land still belonged to Britain, but the fertile land south of the border was all given to Washington. This was in 1782.... [emphasis is in Xu's original]

For the first time in modern history, a high-ranking Chinese official had grasped and conveyed the actual global strategic vulnerability of the British Empire. Worse, for the British, Xu asserts that *George Washington was a greater leader than even the most revered of traditional Chinese rebel heroes:*

> As for Washington, he was an extraordinary man. *In raising a revolt, he was more coura-*

Anson Burlingame's comments to Xu engraved in Chinese characters at the Washington Monument in Washington, D.C.

> *geous than Sheng or Kuang. In carrying out an occupation, he was braver than Ts'ao or Liu. When he took up the three-foot double edged sword and opened up the boundaries for ten thousand li, he did not assume the throne and was unwilling to begin a line of succession. Moreover, he invented a method of selection, a world to be shared by all people, and he swiftly carried out the traditions of the San Dai ("the ancients")....* He governed his states with reverence and respected good customs. He did not esteem military achievements; he was very different from those rulers of other states. I have seen his portrait. His bearing is imposing and excellent. Ah! Can he not be called a hero? ... *of all the famous westerners of ancient and modern times, can Washington be placed in any position but first?* [emphasis in the original]

Xu's argument that Washington's superior leadership qualities surpassed those of traditional Chinese rebel heros is a scathing polemic against the folly of impotent rebellion, versus the durable activity of nation building. The four individuals cited were all popular (almost mythological) historic Chinese rebel-leaders against ruling oligarchical authority. Sheng and Kuang had led the failed peasant revolt against the Qin Dynasty, and Ts'ao Ts'ao and Liu Pei against the Legalist-dominated Han Dynasty. All four of these would later be highly revered by Mao Zedong.

大道之行也天下為公選賢與能講信修睦故人不獨親其親不獨子其子使老有所終壯有所用幼有所長矜寡孤獨廢疾者皆有所養男有分女有歸貨惡其棄於地也不必藏於己力惡其不出於身也不必為己是故謀閉而不興竊亂賊而不作故外戶而不閉是謂大同　孫文

The four words, tian xia wei gong, *are highlighted here.*

But to Xu Jiyu, George Washington had a very different conception of "rebellion," and, instead, *"invented a method of selection, a world to be shared by all people, and he swiftly carried out the traditions of the San Dai."* San Dai refers to the first three Dynasties of recorded Chinese civilization. *"A world to be shared by all people,"* is, in Chinese, the famous classical Confucian idea of *tian xia wei gong*. In its original context, Confucius' use of *tian xia wei gong* was an ancient Chinese version of the General Welfare clause of the U.S. Constitution, central to Confucius' idea of the Great Commonwealth:

> When the Great Dao prevailed, and the *world was shared by all people* [tian xia wei gong], rulers were elected according to their wisdom and ability, and mutual confidence and peace prevailed ... there was no cunning or intrigue and there were no bandits or burglars, and as a result, there was no need to shut one's outer gate at night. This was the period of the Da Tong, or the Great Commonwealth.

In the midst of opium war-era China, governor Xu Jiyu, assisted by the ABCFM's David Abeel, had thus placed the first President of the United States on the level of Confucius and the wisdom of the Chinese ancients. The four characters *tian xia wei gong* would later be engraved on the tomb of Dr. Sun Yat-sen, the revolutionary founder of the first Republic of China.

In *America: New Nations Against Europe,* Xu concludes that:

> The Americans have not established titles of king and count, and they do not follow the rules of succession. The public organs are entrusted to public opinion. There has never been a system of this sort in ancient or modern times. This is really a wonder. . . .

In the section on Latin America, Xu notes that the "ancient state of Mexico" had imitated Washington's new United States in 1810 by rebelling against Spain, followed by Guatemala. Writing about Panama, Xu anticipates events to come:

> Westerners say a canal connecting the oceans can be opened in this land. *If so, the oceans of the east and west will be mixed together as one, and it will be ever so much easier to sail westward to China's eastern border.* [emphasis in original]

The British Counter-Offensive

Only a very small number of Westerners on the scene in the Opium War period were fluent in Chinese and local southern dialects. Abeel, by then a 13-year "veteran" in China, was one of them. Another was Fujian British consul George Tradescant Lay, deemed the "barbarian chief" in Chinese documents of the time. Lay's successor in March 1845 was the infamous Rutherford B. Alcock, whose wife tried to woo Xu with their own "oh so much better than the American" maps of the Western world. Later, Alcock, along with Sir Robert Hart, would become the principal British opponents of American efforts to secure a sovereign China.

Although the 1850 publication of Xu's *A Brief Analysis of the World* was universally celebrated by Chinese nationalists, the most reactionary and corrupt elements within the Manchu Court denounced the work as "not flattering to Chinese prejudices, and moreover valued the companionship of intelligent foreigners."

Their message to Confucian Chinese patriots at the

time was essentially: "If we have made you a Qing official, you can either fight the barbarians to the death, make deals our way, or be deemed a sell-out, and banished from office," like [opium burner] Lin Zexu. In short, some within the Qing establishment detested the very idea of working with Western "friendlies" (like Americans) to buy time to modernize China.

Playing this card accordingly, Lord Palmerston shifted British diplomatic strategy in China in 1850 by initiating official communications with the Qing Court

One can only surmise the utter horror which beset the minds of Chinese-language-literate British operatives of the Opium War era on reading this concluding section of Xu's book.

directly through the new Manchu emperor in Beijing. Palmerston's diplomatic dumping of southern Chinese officials as the Court's historic chief negotiators with Britain achieved its pre-calculated effect; it humiliated and disgraced southern Chinese Confucian officials in the eyes of the Court, providing the pretext to have them all fired. Thenceforth, Xu Jiyu and his Fujian/Canton Chinese pro-American allies were systematically purged.

After an intense political battle, Xu was forced to resign what was one of the most powerful official positions in China at the time. Xu was accused of "selling out to the barbarians," by allowing missionaries (one a medical doctor) to be housed in a Buddhist temple inside the Fuzhou city walls; he simply refused to kick them out. The following is from one of the 1850 memorials Xu sent to Beijing as part of his defense:

> [The British] are island barbarians from the Western Sea... The intractable barbarians having attained their wish [for trade], have become arrogant and their acquisitive desire has not been suppressed.... Cutting them off from trade is like taking a mother's breast from an infant.

In his final defense one month later, Xu continued to insist that the missionaries and their friends were, on the other hand, all "good and peaceful."

Zeng Guofan, Yung Wing, and the 'Self-Strengthening Movement'

Despite his dismissal from official duty, Xu's *A Brief Analysis of the World* would serve for decades as the reference for Chinese patriots in their efforts to liberate China from both colonial domination and foreign instigated separatist rebellions. Confucian nationalist Zeng Guofan (1811-1872), the leader of China's 19th Century "self-strengthening movement," intensively studied Xu's work and became known as the "pro-American" Westernizer of China. Accordingly, Zeng and his collaborators sought to develop a modern Chinese army, create government-regulated industrial enterprises and arsenals, and organize joint U.S.-Chinese educational exchanges. During the period surrounding the American Civil War, Zeng Guofan and his newly-organized Hunan army became the principal obstacle to British/French designs to break up China.

By 1860, the Qing Dynasty Court had come face to face with the brutal reality of an imminent dismemberment of China. After almost a century of brutal Opium trade warfare, the Celestial Empire now lay prostrate, helplessly caught between the combined "pincer movement" of the Confederacy-modeled Taiping rebellion's capture of Nanjing in the South (effectively splitting the country in half), and Lord Elgin's British-French "Arrow Wars" invasion and sacking of Beijing in the North. Manchu China had become a rotting carcass, to be divvied up among foreign competitors and allied regional warlords. Facing catastrophe, the Manchu Court had no choice but to appoint pro-American Viceroy Zeng Guofan as the new imperial commissioner for all of South China. As such, Zeng forged a unified "national army" to suppress the Taiping rebellion. Zeng Guofan, ardent student of *A Brief Analysis of the World*, had now become the most powerful man in all China. Not surprisingly, Zeng went out of his way to secure Yung Wing, the first Chinese to graduate from an American University, as his chief advisor.

At age 13, Yung had been recruited in Macao to attend the Morrison English School by American missionary Rev. S.R. Brown, who later went on to serve with David Abeel's partner, James C. Hepburn, as part of the U.S. Harris Treaty operations to modernize Japan. In 1847, Brown had taken Yung and two other Chinese pupils back to the United States to attend the Monson (Massachusetts) Academy prep-school, where Yung boarded with Brown's mother, coming under the instruction of English literature and Shakespeare enthusiast Rev. Charles Hammond. At Monson, Yung studied physiology and philosophy. When admitted to Yale, Yung insisted on paying his own way through school, rather than accepting financial handouts offered him by influential Brahmin families, all of which came with strings attached. After graduation from Yale, Yung returned to China in the summer of 1855 and took up residence in Canton with Rev. Vrooman of the ABCFM. From 1855-63, he

Zeng Guofan

was employed in a number of different business and merchant enterprises (none of which suited his tastes), including a sortie into Taiping territory, where he met some of its leadership and was severely disappointed with the entire operation.

In 1863, in the midst of the Taiping War and the British-French invasion of northern China, a group of Yung's fellow western-educated friends around Zeng Guofan organized an interview between the two men. Zeng proposed to Yung Wing that he give up all of his business ventures and work full-time in service of the state government, under Zeng's authority. Yung's old Chinese friends, now employed in Zeng Guofan's inner circle, were hell-bent on acquiring machinery from the West to modernize the war and other efforts in China. Yung immediately obliged, seeing this as an opportunity to realize his life-long dream of bringing a full, American-style education to all Chinese people.

In late 1863, Zeng Guofan requested a proposal from Yung for establishing a machine shop near Shanghai, later to became the first modern machine shop in China. In response, Yung proposed:

Yung Win, 1854

>…establishing a mother machine shop, capable of reproducing other machine shops of like character, etc. I especially mentioned the manufacture of rifles, which, I said, required for the manufacture of their component parts separate machinery, but that the machine shop I would recommend was not one adapted for making the rifles, but

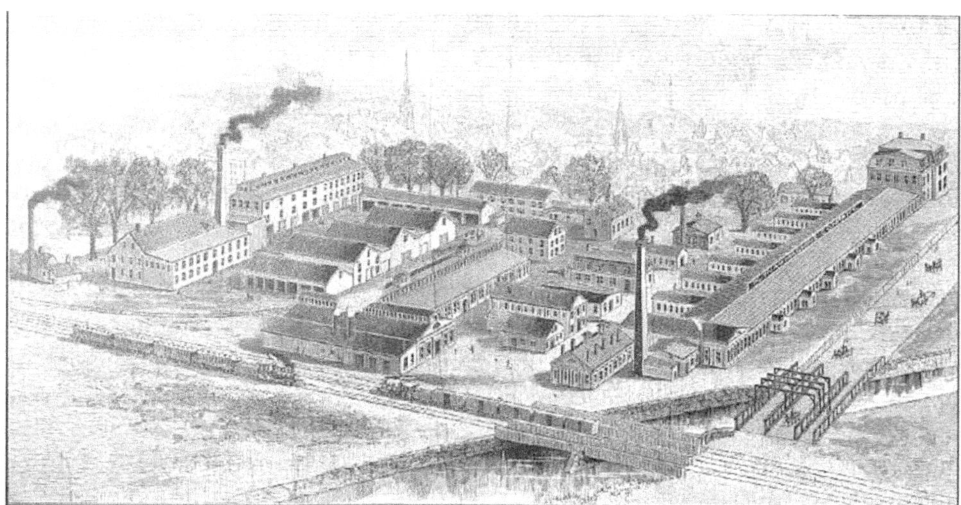

Fitchburg, Mass. Putnam Machinery Co., 1865.

adapted to turn out specific machinery for the making of rifles, cannons, cartridges, or anything else.

Zeng, completely illiterate in any of these matters, immediately commissioned Yung to travel to either England, France or the United States in order to purchase the necessary machinery. Not surprisingly, Yung chose the United States as the location to take his 68,000 Taels of silver for the purchase. Yung's 1864 trip back to the United States was accommodated by American mechanical engineer John Haskins, with whose family Yung traveled the entire journey. While Yung stopped in London to visit a machine shop there, Haskins and family preceded him to New York to work on the specs of the shop machinery desired.

When Yung arrived in New York in the Spring of 1864, Haskins had already secured the relevant purchases from the Putnam Machinery Co. of Fitchburg, Mass. Due to heavy demands from the ongoing American Civil War, all such orders of hardware purchases required a 6-month waiting period. During this time, Yung traveled to Washington, D.C., and *insisted on volunteering his services to the Union army*. The Brigadier General in charge of the Volunteer Department in Washington at the time happened to be from Springfield, Massachusetts, and had remembered meeting Yung at Yale in 1853. After inquiring of Yung's current business in the United States, General Barnes replied, "well, my young friend, I thank you very much for your offer, but since you are charged with a responsible trust to execute for the Chinese government, you had better return to Fitchburg to attend to it."

Victory for the U.S. Constitution and China's Sovereignty

The unprecedented nationalist mobilization of military and economic power required to defeat the 1861-1865 British-backed Confederate insurrection against the American Union, unleashed the greatest explosions of scientific and economic progress in modern history. The Union victory demonstrated to the world that the principles of Hamiltonian economics, applied under republican constitutional law, not only were capable of crushing alien oligarchical enemy attacks, but could also generate unprecedented rates of scientific and technological advances in "promoting the general welfare" of mankind.

In July of 1864, as William Tecumseh Sherman was completing his Atlanta campaign in preparation for the March through Georgia, Zeng Guofan's new army successfully took Nanjing, routing the Taiping. In 1865, Manchu general Senggelinqin was killed by Nienfei rebels. Again, the Qing Court was forced to rely upon Zeng and Li Hongzhang to crush the revolts (accomplished in 1868), further reinforcing the rise in military/civil power of Zeng's Chinese nationalists.

In 1865, the U.S. Hunt Co. sold its entire Shanghai machine and shipyard works to the Chinese Government through Zeng Guofan. Hunt Company chief engineer T.F. Falls, along with eight of his machinists then employed by the New York Novelty Works, were appointed as managers of the Chinese project. By 1867, the new Jiangnan Arsenal was turning out fifteen muskets and one hundred 12-pound shrapnel per day, and eighteen 12-pound howitzers a month. In November 1865, after spending thirteen years in virtual exile in Shanxi, Xu Jiyu received an edict from the Emperor appointing him a member of the Zongli Yamen (the newly created Chinese foreign office) to help supervise affairs between China and foreign states. Also in 1865, Xu wrote the introduction to the long-awaited completion of the first Chinese translation of Euclid's *Elements*, initiated two hundred fifty years before by Matteo Ricci. In February 1867, Xu Jiyu was appointed the first Chinese director of the Tong Wen Guan (Polytechnic School), established in 1862 to train Chinese cadre in Western languages and knowledge in order "to borrow Western methods to verify Chinese methods."

That same year, Yung Wing, chief policy advisor of Xu Jiyu's principal "student" Zeng Guofan, submitted the first concrete historic proposal for advancing the modernization of China to Manchu Prime Minister Wen Xiang. Yung's famous "Four Point Proposal" would become the basis of the historic recognition of China's sovereignty—the Burlingame Treaty of 1868. They were:

1. The organization of a Steamship Company on a joint stock basis. No foreigner was to be allowed to be a stockholder in the company. It was to be a purely Chinese company, managed and worked by Chinese exclusively. Yung described the initiative as an absolutely vital internal improvement of China's infrastructure, required to expedite the transport of food from the South to the North. Later, in 1872, this particular proposal was realized in the creation of the famous China Merchants' Steamship Company. China Merchants' became the model for Chinese government regulated industrial enterprises.

2. Government sponsorship of hand-picked Chinese youths to study abroad to be thoroughly educated for the public service. The scheme contemplated sending one hundred and twenty students to the United States as an experiment. This occurred in 1872, with Yung appointed director of the Chinese Educational Mission, headquartered in Hartford, Connecticut.

3. Induce the government to open the mineral resources of the country and thus introduce railroads to transport the mineral products from the interior to the ports. Forty-five years later, Dr. Sun Yatsen would fully complete this proposal with his unprecedented *International Development of China* blueprint for the full industrialization of China.

4. Prohibit the encroachment of foreign powers upon the independent sovereignty of China by prohibiting missionaries of any sect or denomination from exercising any kind of jurisdiction over their converts, in either civil or criminal cases.

The same year as Yung's proposals, the Chinese Zongli Yamen (the newly created foreign office) had appointed U.S. Secretary of State William Seward's Minister in China, Anson Burlingame, Minister Plenipotentiary of the Empire of China to all Western powers. *An American patriot thus became the first official ambassador of China to the capitals of the modern western world.*

In 1868, Burlingame led his new Chinese embassy to Washington, D.C., via San Francisco. On July 16th, 1868, the United States Senate overwhelmingly ratified the so-called Burlingame Treaty, with the full backing of Secretary of State Seward. For the first time in modern history, the Burlingame Treaty recognized the Government of the Chinese Empire as a sovereign member of the world's Community of Nations. Similar to Townsend Harris' 1858 treaty with Japan, the Burlingame Treaty was an international *coup d'état* against the British oligarchy and her allies.

American republicans, allied with Confucian Chinese nationalists, had successfully secured the recognition of China as a sovereign government, subject to no colonial rule of law. Burlingame's "mission" subsequently traveled to the capitals of Europe, securing similar treaties of recognition. In 1870, China missionary and American patriot William Speer published *The Oldest and the Newest Empire: China and the United States*, a 700-page tour-de-force celebration/promotion of the conception behind the historic breakthrough which was the Burlingame Treaty of 1868.

Speer's work introduced the full sweep of 2,500 years of Chinese customs, culture, language, geography, economy, and history to the wide audience of America's post-Civil War intelligentsia. Speer's included summary of the Burlingame Treaty process correctly identifies its world-historic significance *as an outgrowth of the continuing perfection of the United States Constitution*:

> The treaty defines and fixes the principles of the intercourse of Western nations with China… It secures the territorial integrity of the empire, and concedes to China the rights which the civilized nations of the world accord to each other as to eminent domain over land and waters, and jurisdiction over persons and property therein. It takes the first step toward the appointment of Chinese consuls in our seaports—a measure promotive of both Chinese and American interests. It secures exemption from all disability or

persecution on account of religious faith in either country. It recognizes the right of voluntary emigration and makes penal the wrongs of the coolie traffic. It pledges privileges as to travel or residence in either country such as are enjoyed by the most favored nation. It grants to the Chinese the permission to attend our schools and colleges, and allows us to freely establish and maintain schools in China. And while it acknowledges the right of the Chinese government to control its own whole interior arrangements, as to railroads, telegraphs and other internal improvements, it suggests the willingness of our government to afford aid toward their construction by designating and authorizing suitable engineers to perform the work, at the expense of the Chinese government.

While slavery existed in the United States the Senate would not have ratified a national covenant which accords so freely the rights of equal humanity and equal civilization to a tawny race not of European blood. That covenant will be kept with good faith on our part. It is in harmony with the article of the Constitution recently adopted [the 14th Amendment], which says that no State shall "deprive any person of life, liberty or property without due process of law, nor deny any person within its jurisdiction the equal protection of its laws." *This article we accept as the text of the Constitution of which this treaty is but one example.* It must sweep away the legal disabilities to which the Chinese have been subjected on the Pacific coast, permit them to obtain the sheer rights of humanity, and punish the villains who now plunder, abuse or murder them under the assurance that the testimony of that race will be rejected by the courts. [emphasis added]

America's Manifest Destiny with China

To Speer and many others, the grand design behind the Burlingame Treaty was nothing less than the integration of China, the country with the greatest population and oldest continuous culture on the planet, into the world historic plan of America's Manifest Destiny:

…Bewildering as it is to our ideas, there can be no just exception taken to the computation which makes [China's] population to amount to one-fourth of the entire family of man. It stands first of all existing nations in agriculture productiveness, first in some productive manufacturers, first in the sum of wealth of its subjects. China, to one who can bring his mind to measure what these statements embrace, seems almost a world of itself—a world which, like those strange binary stars which revolve about each other and communicate mutual powerful influences, but are each a distinct sun, has moved all the time, strangely connected with, yet separate from, the world of our ancestry and history.…

It is the appointed office of America to be the ground in which the best benefits of European institutions shall be planted and be improved and indefinitely multiply, by which the toil, the experience and some of the peculiar products of Asia shall assist to enrich and beautify….There shall be a great coming together of nations…which shall cause the heavens to sing, the whole world to be joyful and the mountains to break forth into song of gladness.

On October 21, 1867, just before embarking on his mission as the first ambassador of a sovereign Chinese Empire to the governments of the West, Anson Burlingame presented *A Brief Analysis of the World* author Xu Jiyu, now 72 years old, a copy of Gilbert Stuart's portrait of George Washington. Burlingame's comments to Xu on this historic occasion are probably the finest words ever uttered by a U.S. Government official on the actual nature of America's Manifest Destiny alliance with the best of 4,000 years of Chinese civilization:

It is now nearly twenty years since you published a geographic history of the countries lying beyond the boundaries of China. You brought to the work great labor, a sound judgment, and the marvelous scholarship of your native land. You passed in review the great men of the countries of which you wrote, and placed Washington before all the rest. You not only did this, but you placed him before the statesmen and warriors of your own country, and declared that he recalled the three dynasties whose serene virtues had shed their light along the ages for 4,000 years. Those words have been translated and used by their grateful countrymen of Washington. To show their appreciation of them, the President [Johnson] requested the Secretary of State [Seward] to have made by a distinguished artist this portrait, and to send it over land and sea to be placed in your hands. When you look upon its benignant features, do not recall with sorrow the eighteen [sic] years of retirement endured by you on account of your efforts to make Washington and the countries of the West better known; but rather, exult with us that an enlightened Government has for the same reason placed you near the head of the State, to aid in controlling the affairs of 490,000,000 of people, and what is better by a kind of poetical justice, you have been placed at the head of an institution [the Tong Wen Guan] whose purpose is to advance the views for which you were censured, and to instruct your people in the language and principles of Washington. By doing this, you will please all nations, for Washington belonged not to us alone, but to the world.

His life and character were such as to peculiarly commend him to your countrymen. Like them he honored agriculture; and like them he was for peace, and only fought in defense of his country. Like them, he believed that every man is entitled to the inspiration of fair opportunity, and like them he held to the doctrine of Confucius, spoken 2,300 years ago, "We should not do to others what we would not that others should do to us." This great truth came to Washington, not negatively but positively, from Divinity itself, as a command unto him, "Do unto others as you would have others do unto you." Why should we not exchange our thoughts? Why should we not have the moral maxims of Confucius and Mencius, and you the sublime doctrines of Christianity? Why should we not take your charming manners, your temperance, your habits of scholarship, and your high culture… and you our modern sciences, our railroads and telegraphs, our steamboats? Why should not this great nation, the mother of inventions, whence comes paper, printing, porcelain, the compass, gunpowder and the great doctrine of "The people are the source of power" [Confucius' *Tian xia wei gong*], follow up their inventions and principles, and enjoy them in all their development? Why should not the discoverers of coal have the wealth and strength derived from its use, and those who made the first water-tight vessels guided by a compass, use the great steamers whose swiftness makes us your near neighbors, and which carry a thousand men on their decks? I present this portrait, with all good will, in the name of the people of the United States, hoping it may ever recall to you and yours their enduring friendship for your country, and their love and regard for you, its worthy representative.

Anson Burlingame

Bibliography

Lyndon H. LaRouche, "The Issue of America's Manifest Destiny for Today," *Executive Intelligence Review*; Vol. 27, no. 4, January 28, 2000.

Fred Drake, *China Charts the World: Hsu Chi-yu and his Geography of 1848*, Cambridge; Harvard University Press, 1964.

Yung Wing, *My Life in China and America*. New York; Arno Press, 1978, http://archive.org/details/mylifeinchinaand027665mbp

William Speer, *The Oldest and the Newest Empire: China and the United States*, San Francisco; S.S. Scranton and Co., 1870. http://archive.org/details/cu31924067561559

Korea: Sabotage of LaRouche Plan Brought Slide to Nuclear War

Sept. 4—As the world fearfully watches the powerful North Korean nuclear weapon test, and threats of war from the United States, Lyndon LaRouche reminded the world that it was the sabotage of his "peace through development" policy, first by George Bush and Dick Cheney, and then by Obama, which caused the current crisis. The "Agreed Framework" of 1994 under Bill Clinton was working to end North Korea's nuclear weapons program, with IAEA inspectors on the ground, in exchange for economic cooperation—when Bush and Cheney scrapped it in favor of military threats and confrontation.

EDITORIAL

Again in 2002, when South Korean President Kim Dae-jung proceeded, with backing for his "Sunshine Policy" from Russia and China, to reopen economic cooperation with the North, Bush and then Obama rejected cooperation, while blaming North Korea for "cheating."

The fact is, the British and their neocon cohorts in the United States do not want a solution, since the crisis in Korea justifies their effort to target China, economically and militarily. Indeed, that is made clear today by the response from Washington to the perceived threat from Pyongyang.

The incompetent U.S. Ambassador to the United Nations, Nikki Haley, told today's emergency meeting of the U.N. Security Council that North Korean leader Kim Jong Un is "begging for war," saying that the United States is preparing a draft resolution to be voted on next week, in which "The United States will look at every country that does business with North Korea, as a country that is giving aid to their reckless and dangerous nuclear intentions"—i.e., the target is China, as well as Russia.

Treasury Secretary Steven Mnuchin, the Wall Street asset within the Trump Administration, told Fox News on Sunday that he was working on sanctions such that "Anybody that wants to do trade or business with [North Korea] would be prevented from doing trade or business with us." Presumably he's talking about locking certain Chinese banks and companies out of the U.S. financial system—which is crazy.

This makes it clear that the target is also Trump himself; namely, his efforts to build a working friendship between the United States and both China and Russia, which is the cause of the ongoing "color-revolution" against him by traitors in both parties.

Trump himself tweeted that China is "trying to help but with little success," and accused South Korea of "appeasement" for wanting to engage the North in any way. Gen. Mattis issued a statement saying: "Any threat to the United States, or its territories—including Guam or our allies—will be met with a massive military response, a response both effective and overwhelming."

On the other hand, South Korean President Moon Jae-in's office issued a statement saying: "Korea is a country that experienced a fratricidal war. The destruction of war should not be repeated in this land." Moon has stated clearly that President Trump has assured him that there will be no military action against the North without Seoul's approval. Nonetheless, the Moon government is speeding up the deployment of THAAD missiles in his country (despite strong opposition from China and Russia) and is discussing with Washington the deployment of U.S. strategic military assets in South Korea, including a nuclear-powered aircraft carrier and strategic bombers.

Both China and Russia strongly condemned the North Korean nuclear test, but made clear that Washington's refusal to talk to Pyongyang, or to curtail their military exercises threatening the North, are equally responsible for the crisis. "My personal opinion is that there would have been no conflict at all if the United States stopped maintaining the conflict," Russian Deputy Prime Minister and Presidential Envoy for the Far East Yury Trutnev told Tass. "Every time North and South Korea seem about to come to terms, and tensions start to ease, some naval drills immediately begin, even stipulating a training plan aimed at seizing Pyongyang, which is a direct provocation," Trutnev said.

Chinese Foreign Ministry spokesman Geng Shuang told reporters Monday that North Korea must be very clear that U.N. Security Council resolutions prohibit such activities. But Geng also took exception to the threats against China. He said that China regarded as "unacceptable a situation in which on the one hand we work to resolve this issue peacefully, but on the other hand our own interests are subject to sanctions and jeopardized. This is neither objective nor fair."

China Daily editorialized: "There is no doubt that DPRK's action ... is a gross violation of relevant U.N. Security Council resolutions and has raised serious concerns in the region and worldwide. But Trump is not helping the situation with tweets blasting the DPRK and criticizing South Korea and China." The editorial goes on to argue that "the fundamental failure of Trump's strategy is that it pins too much hope on tightening sanctions, a strategy that has proved a failure for decades." The editorial further argues that "If Trump is right in saying China 'is trying to help but with little success,' it is because the United States has not heeded China's advice, such as resuming the Six-Party Talks, direct contacts between the United States and the DPRK, and accepting 'dual suspension,' in which the United States and South Korea halt their military drills and the DPRK suspends its nuclear tests."

Putin, Xi Jinping, Abe, Moon, and others will be meeting each other this week, some at the ongoing BRICS meeting in Xiamen, and then at the Eastern Economic Forum in Vladivostok, where Korea will be high on the agenda.

Koji

(A Japanese Orphan Boy)

By Jooji Matsumoto

Illustrated by Dan Noyes